Cambridge Elements ☰

Elements in Language, Gender and Sexuality
edited by
Helen Sauntson
York St John University
Holly R. Cashman
University of New Hampshire

LEGAL CATEGORIZATION OF "TRANSGENDER"

An Analysis of Statutory Interpretation of "Sex", "Man", and "Woman" in Transgender Jurisprudence

Kimberly Tao
The Hong Kong Polytechnic University

CAMBRIDGE
UNIVERSITY PRESS

Shaftesbury Road, Cambridge CB2 8EA, United Kingdom

One Liberty Plaza, 20th Floor, New York, NY 10006, USA

477 Williamstown Road, Port Melbourne, VIC 3207, Australia

314–321, 3rd Floor, Plot 3, Splendor Forum, Jasola District Centre,
New Delhi – 110025, India

103 Penang Road, #05–06/07, Visioncrest Commercial, Singapore 238467

Cambridge University Press is part of Cambridge University Press & Assessment,
a department of the University of Cambridge.

We share the University's mission to contribute to society through the pursuit of
education, learning and research at the highest international levels of excellence.

www.cambridge.org
Information on this title: www.cambridge.org/9781009494397

DOI: 10.1017/9781009221221

First published 2024

A catalogue record for this publication is available from the British Library.

ISBN 978-1-009-49439-7 Hardback
ISBN 978-1-009-22120-7 Paperback
ISSN 2634-8772 (online)
ISSN 2634-8764 (print)

Cambridge University Press & Assessment has no responsibility for the persistence
or accuracy of URLs for external or third-party internet websites referred to in this
publication and does not guarantee that any content on such websites is, or will
remain, accurate or appropriate.

Legal Categorization of "Transgender"

An Analysis of Statutory Interpretation of "Sex", "Man", and "Woman" in Transgender Jurisprudence

Elements in Language, Gender and Sexuality

DOI: 10.1017/9781009221221
First published online: February 2024

Kimberly Tao
The Hong Kong Polytechnic University
Author for correspondence: Kimberly Tao, kimberly.tao@cpce-polyu.edu.hk

Abstract: This Element analyzes the foundational frame of legal reasoning when courts interpret the "plain language" and "ordinary meaning" of terms such as "sex," "man," and "woman." There is a rich and complicated line of cases on how to define these terms and how to legally categorize transgender people. When dealing with different legal issues, judges need to give a clear "yes" or "no" determinate answer to a legal question. Marginal categorizations could be problematic even for experts. This Element analyzes nine decisions that relate to transgender people's workplace protection under Title VII in the United States and the right to marry in the United Kingdom and Hong Kong. It brings in a historical discussion of the development of interpretative practices of law and legal categorization of transgender individuals across past decades, drawing on the intricate relationship between time and statutory interpretation.

Keywords: transgender jurisprudence, statutory interpretation, gender ideologies, ordinary meaning, marriage law and Title VII

ISBNs: 9781009494397 (HB), 9781009221207 (PB), 9781009221221 (OC)
ISSNs: 2634-8772 (online), 2634-8764 (print)

Contents

Introduction

Statutory interpretation started to receive legal academics' attention in the early 1980s, with the main emphasis being placed on how the statutes have been construed by different judges and how different legal interpretations could lead to different legal reasonings. As Solan (2010) suggests, analyzing statutory interpretation is one of the ways to learn about the relationship between lawmakers and judges and about judges' decision-making process in different cases. It provides us with a chance to make sense of the seemingly abstract legal reasoning and to trace the formation and progression of legal interpretation across time. It also reveals the different statutory interpretation approaches that the judges adopted when deciding the meaning of the statute. More importantly, learning how different judges construed the same wordings, such as "men" and "women," differently in different cases shows that a single sign could have multiple meanings to different perceivers. It is in this point that indexicality comes to inform us how linguistic signs can carry different layers of indexical meanings, and links between signs and objects can be fluid and can evolve with time (Silverstein, 1985; 2003). Because of its fluid nature, statutory interpretation can also be seen as a form of communication problem because it involves two different parties (the legislators and the judges) who could have different conceptualizations and interpretational practices when reading a statute, resulting in different understandings and negotiations of meanings (Zander, 2004). One could argue that communication problems occur in everyday life, and it is impossible to prevent them from happening. While it is true that communication problems usually occur when two parties are involved, their significance will be much greater when they involve real parties whose legal rights could have been affected by such "communication problems." Hutton (2014a) states that the legal decisions that are made on categories such as race and gender impact radically on individual lives and collective social understanding. The complexities and uncertainties that entail in statutory interpretation could lead the involved parties to face different life-changing legal decisions that could affect their legal functioning and identities in the society.

Recent legal developments relating to transgender protection in the workplace include the US Supreme Court case *Bostock* v. *Clayton County* in 2020, which ruled that Title VII protects homosexual and transgender workers from workplace discrimination. The UK Gender Recognition Act (2004) also allows a qualified transgender person to apply for a full or interim gender recognition certificate. Yet in the background, there is a rich and complicated line of cases on how to define terms such as "sex," "man" and "woman" and how to legally categorize transgender people. When dealing with different legal issues, judges need to give a clear "yes-or-no" determinate answer to a legal question. Yet categorization at the margins could be problematic even for experts, given the many different and complicated situations that can arise. This Element focuses on the legal interpretation and categorization of transgender individuals in law, drawing on cases that concern transgender individuals in the United States, the United Kingdom and Hong Kong (HKSAR). It analyzes nine decisions that relate to transgender people's workplace protection under Title VII in the United States (*Holloway* v. *Arthur Andersen & Co* [1977]; *Ulane* v. *Eastern Airlines, Inc.* [1983] and [1984]; *Smith* v. *City of Salem Ohio* [2004]; *Schroer* v. *Billington* [2008]; *Bostock* v. *Clayton County* [2020]), and the right to marry in the United Kingdom (*Corbett* v. *Corbett* [1971], *Bellinger* v. *Bellinger* [2002] and [2003], *Goodwin* v. *United Kingdom* [2002]) and Hong Kong (HKSAR) (*W* v. *Registrar of Marriages* [2013]). Focusing on statutory interpretation, it explores the foundational frame of legal reasoning when courts interpret the "plain language" and "ordinary meaning" of terms such as "sex," "man," "woman," "male" and "female." Placing the focus of transgender categorization in law allows us to learn about the intricate relationship between law, power and gender ideologies in constructing the circulating (trans)gender understanding and discourse. It brings in a historical discussion of the development of interpretative practices of law and legal categorization of transgender individuals across the past decades. It offers an accessible and analytical guide to legal development of transgender rights In antidiscrimination and marriage law. It aims to find out how transgender individuals have been situated in law throughout history. Such analysis contributes to the legal history of sex and gender and sheds light on how transgender individuals are rejected or accepted by the legal interpretations of the relevant words.

Judges are responsible for making judgments about the scope of legal categories. From a linguistic perspective, learning about the language of a statute and its interpretation process in law can lead us to understand how language works in law and in judges' minds, for such an interpretation process is often related to how judges perceive the ordinary usage of terms in society and in law. Following the framework of indexicality, statutory interpretation can also reflect the stance and ideologies that the judges hold. Statutory interpretation, as this Element will show, often leads us to learn about the establishment, circulation, enforcement and rejection of ideologies in different fields. This Element is intended to present the historical progression of the meaning of "sex," "man" and "woman" in both antidiscrimination and marriage law. It aims to respond to the question as to what definitions and whose definitions the courts are turning to when they face challenges in interpreting who counts as a man and a woman in cases involving transgender people. It also will discuss the impact of precedents on judges' interpretation process, for precedents can serve as a basis for courts to determine cases involving similar issues. This Element also sheds light on how the indexical links between words such as "man" and "woman" and the social meanings (who or what bodies can be considered a "man" or a "woman") were built by judges in specific contexts (Eckert, 2008; Calder, 2021).

1 Intellectual Background

1.1 Understanding Statutory Interpretation in the Common Law System

Statutory interpretation is important in the common law system because common law is not drawn from statutes but rather from legal precedents established by previous courts. A precedent is a history of prior judicial rulings that serve as the standard for future courts to interpret upcoming cases. Judges can decide which precedents should be applied to current cases in hand and to what extent the precedents can be useful and relevant to explaining current cases due to changes in time, context and the nature of the case. Common law has also been described as "puzzling" due to its unpredictable and inconsistent nature in statutory interpretation when compared with the traditional understanding of the rule of law (Melvin, 1988; Schauer, 1989). Such an unpredictable and inconsistent nature can be explained by the following. First, "the rules of the common law are nowhere canonically formulated," and what makes common law rules different from legislative rules is their lack of a single authoritative statement (Schauer, 1989, p. 454). Second, instead of being created by legislatures, common law rules are established by courts during their application of those rules to specific cases (Melvin, 1988; Schauer, 1989). This is to say that courts play an important role in construing the statute in the current context and different interpretations of the statute will then lead to different decisions. More importantly, common law courts have the authority to change or replace a rule that was previously considered to be the law, application of which might lead to malevolent consequences for the situation at hand (Melvin, 1988; Schauer, 1989). The United States (except Louisiana, which is based on the French civil code), Australia, Hong Kong, Canada, England, and India are generally considered to be common law countries, for they were part of the former British Empire.

Concerning the interpretative practice of common law, one of the most fundamental principles is the "plain meaning" or "ordinary meaning" rule (Hutton, 2014b). The "plain meanings" of ordinary words serve as the "default setting of the common law" and judges need to justify their statutory interpretation decisions with legal reasonings if their words deviate from the ordinary meanings (Hutton, 2014b, p. 222). What adds to the "puzzling" elements of common law is its supposedly "essentially universal jurisdiction," one that is not linked to local context or micro-worlds (Hutton, 2014b, p. 222). Against the backdrop of this (quasi-)universal jurisdiction, the English language, regarded as a language that represents an ideal form of English that holds "definitional stability, conceptual transparency, universal applicability and the ability to carry and sustain the coherence of legal reasoning across multiple contexts of application," is the language of common law (Hutton, 2014b, p. 223). One example to be drawn is the legal interpretation of English words under the common law system in Hong Kong and the United Kingdom, which has taken ordinary English words such as "person," "child," "man" and "woman" "for legal purposes as having the same meaning, as are basic legal terms of art such as 'contract', 'trust', 'equity', 'mens rea'" (Hutton, 2014b, p. 224). Such an understanding, nevertheless, does not consider how law and language are restricted by jurisdiction and affected by matters of local belief or practice, causing the supposedly universal applicability of law and universal intelligibility of English to be an imagined or a "conceptual universality" (Hutton, 2014b, p. 224).

The preceding description shows that statutory interpretation in common law is taken to be direct and universal but argued to be complex and restricted to regions and local understandings, resulting in different understandings of the same terms in different jurisdictions. Against the backdrop of the indeterminate and variable natures of statutory interpretation, judges need to come out with a judgment that could be accepted by the community as convincing and legitimate (Solan, 1993). Judges "are engaging in the practice of self-presentation, that is, the practice of offering a persuasive account of why they have done what they have done . . . which is not the same thing . . . as offering an account of how they actually did it" (Fish, 1989, p. 388). Such a "persuasive account" usually would consult a range of sources and styles of reasoning, for instance experts' opinions, legislative history, linguistic analysis, precedents and relevant court cases. As for linguistic analysis, it is often asserted that judges are inconsistent, in that their decisions are sometimes affected by non-linguistic considerations even though linguistic analysis was supposedly the primary reasoning behind the judgment (Solan, 1993). Solan (2010) points out that judges sometimes disagree about what kind of extrinsic evidence to consider when the language does not give a definite answer. Hutton (2014a) also suggests that "law is the master of its own domain" since "judges define their interpretative task and choose the tools and sources of authority that they believe will yield the right answer" (p. 198). Hence, instead of seeing statutory interpretation as universal, this interpretation practice is indeed subject to judges' different understandings of terms and the tools of interpretation that they turned to.

One way of seeing judges' different statutory interpretation practices is through the theoretical framework of indexicality. Being a theoretical concept that is shared by linguistic anthropology and semiotic theory, "indexicality represents a co-occurrence in time and space between a particular sign-vehicle and an object to which the sign-vehicle points" (Calder, 2021, p. 39). The reliance on case precedents as a basis when interpreting the statute shares similarity with the indexicality concept in which signs are being observed and interpreted to co-occur with objects in the past. Under indexicality, linguistic signs can convey the semantic referential meanings and indexical meanings that unveil the speakers' identity, linguistic situation and their stance toward a particular subject (Calder, 2021). Following Silverstein (2003)'s notion of indexical order, Eckert (2008) proposes that "the meanings of variables are not precise or fixed but rather constitute a field of potential meanings – an indexical field, or constellation of ideologically related meanings, any one of which can be activated in the situated use of the variable" (p. 454). When judges are construing the language of a statute, one understanding is that they are selecting the "best" interpretation from the indexical field. Such a selection process has to be understood through the perceiver, for indexical links do not exist in social vacuums (Atkin, 2013; D'Onofrio, 2021; Calder, 2021). Different perceivers may have diverse interpretations of the social meanings that a given linguistic sign corresponds to and one must also attend to context when understanding the indexical links between linguistic signs and objects (Nakassis, 2018). Eckert (2008) also reminds us that the indexical field is fluid and "each new activation has the potential to change the field by building on ideological connections" (p. 454). Given that such a lexical field is subject to changes and signs can index various social meanings and gain new social meanings across time, the interpretation of linguistic signs in law can be seen as fluid instead of universal.

1.2 The Principles of Interpretation, Textualism and Ordinary Meaning

Drawing on the preceding discussion, the key question that this section delves into is how do judges construe the language of the statute? What principles of interpretations are guiding judges to make their decisions? Which approaches are more dominant in cases involving transgender people? When studying constitutional interpretation, there are three approaches that are often introduced to law students, namely literal rule, golden rule and mischief rule, along with a fundamental distinction between literal and "purposive" interpretation (see Zander, 2004; Hutton, 2009). Among these approaches, literal rule received greater attention in the early nineteenth century (Hutton, 2009). Given its significant usage in the specific cases analyzed within this Element, the literal rule will be expllred in greater detail dIe to its substIntial impact on shaping the outcomes of those cases. In general, the literal rule deals with the statutory meaning itself, irrespective of its intention or purposes. Zander (2004) explains it as "the task of the court to give the words to be construed their literal meaning regardless of whether the result is sensible or not" (p. 130). Lord Eshor (1892) puts it as follows: " If the words of an Act are clear, you must follow them, even though they lead to a manifest absurdity. The court has nothing to do with the question whether the legislature has committed an absurdity."[1]

For the literal rule, the task of interpreting the language of the statute should be kept simple and straightforward. Judges should follow the direct meaning of the statute without considering other nontextual factors, such as legislative intent and the possible absurd consequences that might follow. This approach has been widely used by the judges because its assertion seems to allow the task of statutory interpretation to stand against time and space. Judges from different periods and regions should be able to reach approximately identical decisions by interpreting the plain language of the statute.

After learning the key principle of interpretation in law, this section intends to discuss two main strands of statutory interpretation: textualism and purposivism. Both textualists and purposivists place the importance on the context that a statute should be interpreted in. However, the contexts that they value differ, for textualists stress a statute's "semantic context" and pay attention to a reasonable person's understanding of statutory language in context, while purposivists emphasize its "policy context" and the purpose and intent of the legislature (Manning, 2006; Fallon Jr, 2014, p. 685). The different takes that both approaches have on statutory interpretation show that the selection of context is significant in determining the interpretation of the statutory language. As the following sections will show, the courts in transgender-related cases mainly are concerned with the plain language and the ordinary meaning of the words "sex," "man" and "woman." What follows, therefore, first highlights the legal practice of judges in searching for the "plain and ordinary meaning" of terms through the discussion of textualism. For textualists, courts involved in statutory interpretation should not be turning to sources other than the plain meaning of the statute. The main principle of textualism is to ensure that citizens

---

[1] *R. v. Judge of the City of London Court* [1892] 1 QB 273 at 290.

can read the statute books and know their rights and duties (Eskridge, 1994). Based on this rule, it asserts that the statutory language should be read on its literal meaning. As Solan (2010) puts it, "[t]he goal of the textualist program is to reach results in disputed cases that are sensitive to a statute's purpose, and thus respectful of the primacy of the legislature, without resorting to extratextual materials that create both evidentiary and conceptual difficulties" (p. 52). United States Supreme Court Justice Antonin Scalia has long been known as one of the dominant figures who adopted the textualist approach in legal reasoning. His textualist approach addresses the significance of context for word meaning and focuses on the search for the ordinary meaning of statutory words (Solan, 2010). He also rejects mischief rules or other purposive approaches. To Scalia, it is crucial to be loyal to the language of the statute (Scalia, 1997). When searching for the ordinary meaning, textualists tend to suggest that one should pay attention to the meaning that stands out and pops up in ordinary people's minds. However, it has been argued that the finding of such ordinariness in ordinary meaning is sometimes a difficult task and the inconsistency that entails in this approach might, to a certain extent, reduce the uniformity of the law (see Hutton, 2009; Solan, 2010). In addition, meanings of words can change over time and the textualist approach may have suggested a rather simplistic connection between the linguistic signs and indexical meanings, one that fails to address the context, fluidity and complexity in the meaning derivation process. In a Hong Kong case, *Cheng Kar Shun* v. *Li Fung Ying* (2009 at 103),[2] Judge Andrew Cheung made the distinction between textualist and purposive approaches: " The Basic Law must not be read with a literal, technical, narrow or rigid approach. It must be given a purposive interpretation, which fully takes into account the context and purpose of the relevant provisions."

Justice Cheung points out that the textualist approach is a "narrow" and "rigid" one that fails to consider the context and purpose of the statute. The purposive approach, on the other hand, can fill in the gap and leads the court to a more comprehensive and sensible interpretation of the statutory language for the case.

To understand the debate on the limitations of textualism, it is important to learn about the challenges that textualists could face when using dictionaries to make sense of the statutory language. The dictionary is one of the most cited sources of reference when judges are dealing with the ordinary meaning of the words in statute. Since Justice Scalia's appointment in 1986, the references to dictionary definitions have increased, with Scalia himself being one of the

---

[2] *Cheng Kar Shun* v. *Li Fung Ying* [2009], para. 103.

supporters (Solan, 2010). One important case that looks at literal meaning is *John Angus Smith* v. *United States* (1993), a case that demonstrated how two potential literal meanings were in conflict. The defendant Smith offered to trade an automatic weapon for cocaine and was then arrested by an undercover police officer. Title 18 USI S 924(c)(1) penalizes a defendant who "during and in relation to [a] drug trafficking crime uses ... a firearm." The Court of Appeals in this case upheld Smith's conviction and sentence, given that the "plain language" did not contain a meaning that the firearm needs to be used as a weapon. The court ruled that trading the firearm was one of the ways of "using" a firearm. The Supreme Court upheld the decision by quoting dictionary definitions from Webster's (2nd edition, 1939) and *Black's Law Dictionary* (6th edition, 1990) to support its claim that "to use" includes various meanings such as "to employ," "to utilize" and "to derive service from." The words "as a weapon," however, did not appear in the statute:

> Had Congress iInded S924(c)(1) to require proof that the defendant not only used his firearm but used it in a specific manner – as a weapon – it could have so indicated in the statute. However, Congress did not. The fact that the most familiar example of "us[ing] ... a firearm" is "use" as a weapon does not mean that the phrase excludes all other ways in which a firearm might be used.[3]

Justice Scalia, however, wrote a dissenting judgment (in a court which divided 6–3), which also addressed the ordinary usage of the phrase "to use." He cited the analogy of using a cane as an adornment in the hallway to point out that some types of "uses" simply are beyond the normal usage of the verb:

> When someone asks "Do you use a cane?" he is not inquiring whether you have your grandfather's silver handled walking stick on display in the hall; he wants to know whether you walk with a cane. Similarly, to speak of "using a firearm" is to speak of using it for its distinctive purpose, i.e., as a weapon. To be sure, "one can use a firearm in a number of ways" ..., including as an article of exchange, just as one can "use" a cane as a hall decoration – but that is not the ordinary meaning of "using" the one or the other.[4]

From the dissenting judgment, one can learn that Scalia has distinguished possible usage (using a cane as a hall decoration) from ordinary usage (using a cane as a walking stick) and held that only ordinary meaning should be considered by the court when interpreting a statute. The preceding *Smith* case shows that even by applying the same textualist approach, judges can still reach

[3] *John Angus Smith* v. *United States* [1993], para. 229.
[4] *John Angus Smith* v. *United States* [1993], para. 242.

different decisions on finding its most "ordinary" meaning. Whether to seek reference from a dictionary to interpret a statute's language and to what extent dictionary definitions can represent such ordinary usage will then be matters of central concern. This further suggests that by holding different interpretations of the literal meaning of the phrase "uses . . . a firearm," the judges of the majority judgment and Scalia of the dissenting judgment were building different indexical links in which context is playing an important role in the phrase's construction. They were drawing different meanings of the pIrase from the indexical field, representing the perceivers' different construal of the connection between the sign and an object (Gal & Irvine, 2019). Werbach (1994) is skeptical about the proposition that dictionary definitions are "neutral" and "reductive" and that they can be used as admissible evidence in court. Justice Holmes's opinion in *Gompers* v. *United States* also denies that dictionaries can tackle provisions of the constitution:

> [T]he provisions of the Constitution are not mathematical formulas having their essence in their form; they are organic, living institutions transplanted from English soil. The[ir] significance is vital, not formal; it is to be gathered not simply by taking the words and a dictionary, but by considering their origin and the line of their growth.[5]

A similar view was expressed by Justice Brennan in his dissenting opinion in *Lyng* v. *Northwest Indian Cemetery Protective Ass'n*, which stated that "the dictionary is hardly the final word on the meaning of constitutional language."[6] Aprill (1998) also noted that language was constantly changing and this made dictionaries often out of date by the time they were published. Rynd (1991) addresses the space and cost limitations of dictionaries and argues that such limitations make it difficult for dictionaries to assert completeness or perfection in representing word meanings. Dictionaries are seen as selective and incomprehensive in this sense. The dictionary itself is indeterminate and general, and in many cases provides various definitions for judges to select in the process of legal interpretation. Dictionaries are supposed to capture how people use words since they are designed to record how words are used by those who use them. Hence, it seems somewhat circular to use dictionaries as an objective standard to dictate how people should interpret language. To use dictionary definitions to represent the ordinary meaning of the statute, Aprill (1998) argues, is to merely use them to provide "generalizations, summaries, and approximations." Cunningham et al. (1993) also question the usage of dictionaries, for they can never replace the role of linguists in linguistic interpretation: "unfortunately,

---

[5] *Gompers* v. *United States* [1914] 233 US para. 604.
[6] *Lyng* v. *Northwest Indian Cemetery Protective Ass'n* [1988] 485 US 438.

compared to the analysis of a particular textual problem used by a trained linguist, dictionaries are a crude and frequently unreliable aid to word meaning and usage" (p. 1563). In addition, it is often asserted that judges are inconsistent, in that their decisions are sometimes affected by nonlinguistic considerations even though linguistic analysis was supposedly the primary reasoning behind the judgment (Solan, 1993). Judges sometimes also tactically use dictionaries to support their decisions because they can offer authority that seems "objective and general" (Hutton, 2009, p. 101) and make law appear to be more democratic (Hutton, 2014a).

1.3 Linguistic Indeterminacy and Dynamic Interpretation

One of the major challenges for textualists is to prove that a consistent and fixed interpretation on "plain language" exists across different times and places. Doubts, however, have been cast on such attempts because language has been argued as indeterminate and heterogeneous. According to Hutton (2019a), "[i]ndeterminacy implies movements: relationships between texts, readers and contexts are in motion, and there is no one point of view of interpretative position from which a single meaning can be assigned" (p. 40). Deleuze and Guttari (1988) state that "[s]ince everybody knows that language is heterogeneous, variable reality, what is the meaning of the linguists' insistence on carving out a homogeneous system in order to make scientific study possible?" (pp. 100–101). Rather than holding that language is static, fixed and homogeneous, language is known to be reflexive and dynamic. "Language is reflexive in that it can be 'turned back' upon itself, and includes a complex vocabulary for talking about, or referring to, itself" (Hutton, 2009, p. 42). Linguistic or non-linguistic signs, according to Harris (1998), are intrinsically indeterminate. Language evolves with time and opens up the possibility for the statute to be interpreted in the present here and now. Eskridge (1994) argues that universal objectivity simply cannot be achieved through interpretation because interpreters' own context and background influence the act of interpretation and their own perspectives will often interact with the text and historical context. He further suggests that statutory interpretation is always a form of "dynamic interpretation" because "statutory interpretation is multifaceted and evolutive rather than single-faceted and static, involves policy choices and discretion by the interpreter over time as she applies the statute to specific problems, and is responsive to the current as well as the historical political culture" (p. 48). The futurity of statutes has been stressed in his work, for statutes' indefinite life should allow them to be applied in the future and in different situations. Such dynamic interpretation occurs especially when the statute fails to resolve controversial issues. This is because it gives room for the law to respond to changes of time and for the interpreter to exercise discretion to avoid interpreting the statute in ways that might not have been expected by its original authors (Eskridge, 1994).

1.4 Hard Cases and Fuzzy Boundaries

Legal philosopher H. L. A. Hart's legal theory contributes significantly to the understanding of the category in ordinary language. Hart holds that legal rules have to be formulated in terms of general categories of ordinary language given that "the law must predominantly . . . refer to classes of person, and to classes of acts, things, and circumstances" and that law has to depend on "a widely diffused capacity to recognize particular acts, things, and circumstances as instances of the general classifications which the law makes" (Hart, 1994, p. 124). For "instances of the general classifications" he suggests that there are certain events and things that presumably can be recognized as part of the instances of a legal category by the law. There are "plain cases constantly recurring in similar contexts to which general expressions are clearly applicable" (Hart, 1994, p. 126). These are cases where categorization seems simple and "the general terms seem to need no interpretation" and "the recognition of instances" is generally treated as "unproblematic" or "automatic." He termed those cases as "plain cases," and those cases can be determined within the core meaning of the statute (Hart, 1994). However, there were also hard cases where the object involved in the legal question could bring uncertainties and an "unproblematic" answer could not be easily generated. Under such circumstances, more efforts will then be spent by judges on solving the problem of legal categorization and yielding an answer to the ordinary meaning of the statute. Hart (1994) discusses both cases with the example of "vehicle" given that "moto-car" is a clear example of the category of "vehicle" while "bicycles, airplane, roller skaters" are unclear examples of it (p. 126). One of the reasons for such a categorical conundrum is because of the fuzzy boundaries of the terms.

Solan (1995) sheds light on the categorization process by suggesting that human beings usually form categories by "absorbing prototypes, and that concepts become indeterminate at the margins" (p. 1073). Even though prototype theory fails to provide a full explanation of the formation of all categories, it plays a significant role in legal categorization and the construction of ordinary meaning in law (Solan, 2010). Wittgenstein (1978 contends that the functioning of categorical practices only turns problematic when there are concerns over category boundaries. This is because such thinking violates the idea that people can "deal with categories on the basis of clear cases in the total absence of information about boundaries" (Rosch, 1999, p. 196). Those categories on fuzzy boundaries will then bring uncertainties and challenges to the core of categorization. In response to this, questions such as "what principles determine which items will be judged the more prototypical and what other variables might be affected by prototypicality" will then be asked (Rosch, 1999, p. 197). Because of the existence of fuzzy boundaries, categorization is understood as involving induction, intuition, and an inevitable degree of indeterminacy (Solan, 1993). When confronted with important questions regarding categorization, people tend to consult experts about concepts on categorization and suppose that problems will be solved with the help of their expertise (Solan, 1993). Yet categorization at the margins could be problematic even for experts, given the many different and complicated situations that can arise. Their expertise could also be insufficient and irrelevant to the categorical problem that we are facing in the law (Solan, 1993). The following section will discuss the historical background and relationship betIeen law and transgender individuals, individuals who are constanIly on "fuzzy boundaries" in the eyes of the law and pose questions concerning the legal interpretation of terms such as "sex," "man," "woman," "male" and "female."

1.5 Understanding Law and Transgender Individuals

The term "transgender" is an umbrella category that encompasses all gender variance (Bolin, 1994). By encompassing all gender variance, it encompasses all gender possibilities. These gender possibilities, however, are what the modern world disfavors since they destabilize the stable and make governing difficult. The strict insistence on confining categorical order and maintaining social control can be found in the social and legal fields (Latour, 1993; Foucault, 1978; Hutton, 2019b). However, the seemingly fixed categories like man/woman and natural/artificial have been constantly challenged by the existence of "hybrids" (Latour, 1993) and other "form(s) of categorical ambiguity" (Foucault, 1980, p. viii). One example is that law is facing challenges when it has to deal with a category such as "transgender" that challenges the binary gender distinction and decide where to draw the line when answering questions regarding what counts as a man and a woman as well as who deserves protection and treatment in law. Law in general holds to a binary theory of sex and gender, and for many purposes maintains a strict distinction between a man and a woman. The definitions and conceptualizations of "sex," "man" and "woman," however, vary across time. In the early twentieth century, these terms were highly related to the manifestations of psychological, physical, social and behavioral characteristics (Weiss, 2008). This can be shown by the following quotes from Justice Bradley concurring in *Bradwell* v. *Illinois* (1872), a decision that denied Myra Bradwell admission to the Illinois bar because she was a woman:

> The natural and proper timidity and delicacy which belongs to the female sex evidently unfits it for many of the occupations of civil life . . . . [T]he domestic sphere [is] that which properly belongs to the domain and functions of womanhood . . . . The paramount destiny and mission of woman are to fulfil [sic] the noble and benign offices of wife and mother. This is the law of the Creator . . . .
>
> The humane movements of modern society, which have for their object the multiplication of avenues for woman's advancement, and of occupations adapted to her condition and sex, have my heartiest concurrence. But I am not prepared to say that it is one of her fundamental rights and privileges to be admitted into every office and position, including those which require highly special qualifications and demanding special responsibilities. . . . [I]n view of the peculiar characteristics, destiny, and mission of woman, it is within the province of the legislature to ordain what offices, positions, and callings shall be filled and discharged by men, and shall receive the benefit of those energies and responsibilities, and that decision and firmness which are presumed to predominate in the sterner sex.[7]

The preceding quotes show that when describing the female sex, the court did not make reference to Myra Bradwell's biological sex (such as genitalia, chromosomes) but to her gender role functioning as "the noble and benign offices of wife and mother." Some of Bradwell's personal characteristics that were perceived by the court as "timidity and delicacy" made her a natural woman who failed to showcase her suitability for the job that was once deemed as suitable only for men. Her lack of "energies and responsibilities" as well as "decision and firmness" also made her fall under the category of "woman." While this case does not appear to reflect a fundamental difference between one's sex and gender, the stereotypical understanding of these concepts started to shift when scientists began exploring the biological bases of sex characteristics. Two significant moves came from the discovery of sex chromosomes in the early 1900s and the establishment of the role of sex hormones in the late 1920s (Schwartz, 2009). These discoveries enabled the world to see "sex," "man" and "woman" from different perspectives – perspectives that value scientific justification of one's sex and maintain a binary gender distinction.

Foucault (1978) points out that the juridical system of power produces its own subjects and defines how they were represented and classified. In *Ashlie* v. *Chester-Upland School District* (1979), the court drew an analogy between

---

[7] *Bradwell* v. *Illinois*, 83 US 130, 141–142 [1872].

transgender people and donkeys when supporting its conclusion that the right to privacy does not protect school teacher Jenell Ashlie, a transgender woman assigned male at birth, from termination.[8]

> It might just as easily be argued that the right of privacy protects a person's decision to be surgically transformed into a donkey. *The transformation, by its very happening, would lose the quality of privateness.* Certainly, those who had known the donkey as a man would detect the change, even though those acquainted only with the donkey might never have occasion to remark upon it. In addition, the change from man to beast might be just as devoutly wished, as psychologically imperative, and as medically appropriate as the change from man to woman, but the Constitution, I fear, could no long bear the weight of such an interpretation.[9] (emphasis added)

The perceived abnormality and awkwardness that lay behind the transgender plaintiff's transformation led the judge to view her as something that is less than human and more as an animal and a beast. For the court, there is no difference between the surgically created donkey and a human being who is marked by one's humanity. The transgender plaintiff's transformation is something that the judge could not comprehend given that "the change from a man to a woman" to him was no different from "man to beast."[10] It is also the "abnormal" transformation that the plaintiff took which caused her to "lose the quality of privateness."[11] This is to deny transgender people's personhood in the eyes of law. It is apparent that the transformation is what counted as problematic and abnormal, and constituted the plaintiff's monstrousness from the court's point of view. This also caused her to be seen as less than human and not to enjoy the legal recognition and protection that human beings deserve. Foucault notes that law has a "monster" category that represents "the transgression of natural limits" (as cited in Sharpe, 2010, p. 32). Transgender individuals, in this sense, represent an example of "nature gone awry" because of their desire for gender and bodily transformation (Sharpe, 2010, p. 92). They also represent a breach of law for they challenge legal taxonomy and certitude which could thereby challenge the rigid boundary of "man" and "woman" that law seeks to maintain (Sharpe, 2010). Goodrich (1996) suggests that "the substantive rules and doctrinal interpretations of [marriage] contracts manifest a very strict set of images of gender and of the relationships within and between the genders" (p. 19). Transgender individuals have been regarded as turning important legal

---

[8] *Ashlie v. Chester-Upland School District.*, No. 78–4307 [US DDC 1979], paras. 14–15. (The court held that a transsexual may not seek protection under the privacy doctrine from a state government employer's job discrimination.)

[9] *Ashlie v. Chester-Upland School District.*, No. 78–4307 [US DDC 1979], paras. 14–15.

[10] *Ashlie v. Chester-Upland School District.*, No. 78–4307 [US DDC 1979].

[11] *Ashlie v. Chester-Upland School District.*, No. 78–4307 [US DDC 1979].

questions into "uncertain and undecidable," challenging the unchallengeable nature of law that is embedded in its categorical structures (Sharpe, 2010, p. 33). Judges, in this case, hold the authority to decide the categorical answer to transgender individuals' legal gender role. The different sources of authority that they draw on in the process of deciding the "legal sex" of the transgender individuals involved can largely decide whether the individuals can receive recognition and the legal rights that they fought for. As Butler (1993) suggested, "the construction of the human is a differential operation that produces the more and the less 'human', the inhuman and the humanly unthinkable" (p. 8). Law, in this sense, contributes to the notion of who counts as a "legitimate" human being in a specific and cultural moment.

Having conceptualized the juridical field as a "social space," Bourdieu (1987) suggests that law serves as a platform for direct conflict between different parties to be converted into a debate that is juridically regulated between different legal actors (see also Smith, 2000). When dealing with categorical challenges that are brought by transgender individuals, judges are situated in a web of sources of authority that provide different perceptions on the construction of one's sex. Such sources include dictionaries, expert opinions, legislative intent, precedents, and court cases in other jurisdictions. Whether a transgender individual's sex can be legally recognized will then be a matter of how the judges interact with these different parties and contribute to the existing (trans)gender discourse in law. The statutory interpretation plays a significant role in the establishment of a given (trans)gender identity in law and the individuals' conceptualization of the notions of self, power, and body. The power of the norm, medicine and law that see biology as the "ultimate truth," leads one to view certain bodies and genital statuses as "wrong" and certain statuses as deviant, thereby contributing to the formation of different kinds of discrimination (Hooley, 1994). Certain bodies that do not fall into the legal understanding of "legitimate" bodies can be trapped in fixed categories that are upheld by the law and lead to categorical collapse. For them, their gender identities will be treated as illegitimate and incomprehensible from the legal perspective. Foucault denies the idea of having an autonomous agentive subject because the accountability that law seems to attribute to the subject is believed to be illusory (Hutton, 2009). Transgender people, in this sense, can be seen as playing a passive role in the issue of legal definition and classification for they are controlled by the coercive language of the law and the law is operating as an autonomous discourse that causes law to make us, just as "language speaks us" (Hutton, 2009, p. 116). They also have very limited or even no control over the legal interpretation on the relevant terms and legal classification of their sex.

The following discussion analyzes the legal interpretation and categorization of transgender individuals in antidiscrimination law in the United States and in marriage law in the United Kingdom and Hong Kong (HKSAR). It analyzes nine decisions that relate to transgender people's workplace protection under Title VII in the United States (*Holloway* v. *Arthur Andersen & Co* [1977]; *Ulane* v. *Eastern Airlines, Inc.* [1983] & [1984]; *Smith* v. *City of Salem Ohio* [2004]; *Schroer* v. *Billington* [2008]; *Bostock* v. *Clayton County* [2020]), and the right to marry in United Kingdom (*Corbett* v. *Corbett* [1971], *Bellinger* v. *Bellinger* [2002], [2003], *Goodwin* v. *United Kingdom* [2002]) and Hong Kong (HKSAR) (*W* v. *Registrar of Marriages* [2013]). These cases mainly concern transgender women assigned male at birth who faced discrimination in the workplace due to their (trans)gender identities (Title VII cases) and whose affirmed gender identity has failed to be recognized under the marriage law. These cases were selected for this Element because they have been discussed and quoted in one another and have set precedents or been seen as referencing points for the later cases. Both rights to work under the legal protections against discrimination and rights to marry in one's affirmed gender identity are fundamental to transgender individuals' legal and social recognition of their gender identity and social functioning. A cross-reading of cases within the US antidiscrimination law (Title VII) and the United Kingdom and Hong Kong's marriage law can present a picture of the historical development of transgender individuals' legal categorizations and status in two of the most important domains in establishing one's (gender) identity. Both US and UK law dealt with one of their first cases involving transgender individuals in the 1970s and have ever since set an influential precedent respectively for the following cases that concern transgender individuals. Sections 2 and 3 discuss the biological sex approach that the *Holloway* and *Corbett* courts had adopted, and their influences on how transgender individuals were categorized and understood in the following forty years. Against Hong Kong's British colonial historical backdrop, Hong Kong (HKSAR) is a common law jurisdiction within the People's Republic of China (PRC) and adopts a bilingual (Chinese and English) common law system. Hong Kong's unique historical and legal backgrounds further add to the complexities for transgender individuals to be understood and categorized in law. Section 3 therefore further analyzes how Hong Kong courts construe the meanings of "man" and "woman" in marriage law. As the discussion shows, judges in these cases often resort to the search for "plain," "ordinary meaning" of the terms "sex," "man," and "woman" and resorted to different sources of authorities in such a process, resulting in different decisions. This Element further argues that the search for "ordinary" meanings often reflects dominant ideologies, and has a strong tendency to keep stigmatized people stigmatized, as reflected in the judges' statutory interpretation practices. Concerning the terminologies used in this Element, the term "transgender" has been chosen to encompass a variety of gender identities and expressions and it is used throughout the whole discussion. Terms such as "transsexual" or "transsexualism" are only used when they were used in relevant court cases.

2 Legal Categorization and Definition of the Term "Sex" in Title VII

2.1 Introduction

Focusing on the process of searching for the "plain" and "ordinary meaning" of the statute, this section examines transgender people's legal status and protection at the workplace under Title VII of the Civil Rights Act of 1964. Title VII provides that discrimination against any individual with respect to compensation, terms, conditions, or privileges of employment because of such individual's race, color, religion, sex, or national origin would be regarded as an unlawful employment practice.[12] As noted by US Supreme Court justice William Rehnquist, the "prohibition against . . . discrimination based on sex was added to Title VII at the last minute on the floor of the House of Representatives."[13] Due to the last-minute addition, "we are left with little legislative history to guide us in interpreting the Act's prohibition against discrimination based on 'sex.'"[14] Because of this "last-minute addition" and an absence of a statutory interpretation of the term "sex," judges are then responsible for interpreting the term "because of . . . sex" in Title VII. To establish a case of discrimination, a plaintiff must show: (1) she is a member of a protected class, (2) she was qualified for her position, (3) she suffered an adverse employment action, and (4) others similarly situated, but outside the protected class, were treated more favorably.[15] This section intends to unpack the statutory interpretation process of the term "because of . . . sex" and to find out the linguistic resources that judges drew on when dealing with legal questions that might be perceived by some to be on the fuzzy boundaries.

---

[12] Title VII of the Civil Rights Act of 1964, 42 USC § 2000e-2(a)(1) 2006.

[13] *Meritor Sav. Bank, FSB* v. *Vinson*, 477 US 57, 64–64 [Supreme Court, 1986].

[14] *Meritor Sav. Bank, FSB* v. *Vinson*, 477 US 57, 64–64 [Supreme Court, 1986].

[15] *Lopez* v. *River Oaks Imaging & Diagnostic Group*, 542 F.Supp.2d 653 [S.D.Tex. 2008], p. 653.

2.2 Cases Analysis

2.2.1 Restricting the Term "Sex" to Its "Traditional Meaning"

This section begins with two cases that concluded that transgender plaintiffs were not a protected group under Title VII for discrimination. Both the Seventh and Ninth Circuits ruled that Title VII did not include transgender discrimination and concluded that such a case can only be established if and only if the transgender plaintiffs were discriminated against on the basis of being male or female.

Holloway v. Arthur Andersen & Co. [1977]

Holloway v. *Arthur Andersen & Co.* is one of the first cases involving employment discrimination under Title VII that was brought by a transgender plaintiff. The plaintiff, Holloway,began to receive female hormone treatments one year after she entered the company and then received a promotion. However, after having informed her supervisor about her usage of hormones and her plan to undergo transitioning surgery, one company official "suggested that [Holloway] would be happier at a new job where her transsexualism would be unknown" on her annual review in 1974.[16] Her job termination notice also arrived after she had requested a change to her company records to reflect her new first name. Given these circumstances, she filed a sex discrimination claim, alleging that she was terminated because of her transgender identity.[17] The District Court first held that Title VII did not include transgender discrimination. The Ninth Circuit then affirmed the District Court's decision and declared that "[the] term 'sex' should be given its traditional definition based on the anatomical characteristics which divide organisms into males and females."[18] The judge quoted the definition from *Webster's Seventh New Collegiate Dictionary* that defines "sex" as "either of two divisions of organisms distinguished respectively as male or female."[19] The Court of Appeal also concluded that statute should be given its plain meaning and the traditional meaning of "sex" should be the only meaning that Congress had in mind when they drafted the Act. Apart from adopting the plain-meaning approach, the Court also looked at the "manifest purpose" of Title VII and held that the Act is to "assure that men and women were treated equally."[20] The Court ruled that since there is no proof that congressional intent of the term "sex" can be expanded beyond its traditional

---

[16] *Holloway* v. *Arthur Andersen & Co.*, 566 F. 2d 659, 661 [9th Cir. 1977], para. 661.

[17] *Holloway* v. *Arthur Andersen & Co.*, 566 F. 2d 659, 661 [9th Cir. 1977], para. 661.

[18] *Holloway* v. *Arthur Andersen & Co.*, 566 F. 2d 659, 661 [9th Cir. 1977], para. 661.

[19] *Holloway* v. *Arthur Andersen & Co.*, 566 F. 2d 659, 661 [9th Cir. 1977], para. 662.

[20] *Holloway* v. *Arthur Andersen & Co.*, 566 F. 2d 659, 661 [9th Cir. 1977], para. 663.

meaning (i.e. "cisgender man" and "cisgender woman"), people who undergo gender transition therefore could not be a protected class under Title VII.[21] In short, Holloway failed to establish a case under Title VII that she was discriminated against as a transgender person but not as a male or female person.

In a dissenting judgment from the Court of Appeals, Circuit Judge Goodwin interpreted the language of the statute to protect the plaintiff.[22] Judge Goodwin argued that "when a transsexual completes his or her transition from one sexual identity to another, that person will have a sexual classification."[23] He stated that whether the employer had discharged the plaintiff due to the fact that the employee was in surgery or had completed the surgery, the discharge would still have to be classified as one based upon sex.[24] It was irrelevant to the judge whether the plaintiff was assigned female at birth or born intersex (e.g. with atypical genitalia) and raised and socialized as female.[25] More importantly, the judge found that because the plaintiff was a purported female on the day she was fired, she was then a member of the class of protection under Title VII.[26]

Ulane v. *Eastern Airlines, Inc.* [1983] & [1984]

After *Holloway*, the case *Ulane* v. *Eastern Airlines, Inc.* (*Ulane I*) was delivered in 1983, concerning the right of a transgender person who had undergone gender confirmation surgery to be protected. The plaintiff worked as a pilot for Eastern Airlines. The plaintiff wished to live as a woman and underwent sex reassignment surgery (a term that was used in the case) after serving more than ten years at the company. After the company learned about her surgery, the plaintiff was fired in 1981. This case brought significant impact to transgender legal protection because it alleged that Eastern Airlines discriminated against Karen Frances Ulane as a transgender person and simply as a female person.[27] The District Court in *Ulane I* first ruled in favor of Ulane by stating that Title VII of the Civil Rights Act of 1964 should apply to transgender individuals. Title VII, from the judge's point of view, should be viewed as a remedial statute that

---

[21] *Holloway* v. *Arthur Andersen & Co.*, 566 F. 2d 659, 661 [9th Cir. 1977], para. 663.

[22] *Holloway* v. *Arthur Andersen & Co.*, 566 F. 2d 659, 661 [9th Cir. 1977] (Judge Goodwin, dissenting), para. 664.

[23] *Holloway* v. *Arthur Andersen & Co.*, 566 F. 2d 659, 661 [9th Cir. 1977] (Judge Goodwin, dissenting), para. 664.

[24] *Holloway* v. *Arthur Andersen & Co.*, 566 F. 2d 659, 661 [9th Cir. 1977] (Judge Goodwin, dissenting), para. 664.

[25] *Holloway* v. *Arthur Andersen & Co.*, 566 F. 2d 659, 661 [9th Cir. 1977] (Judge Goodwin, dissenting), para. 664.

[26] *Holloway* v. *Arthur Andersen & Co.*, 566 F. 2d 659, 661 [9th Cir. 1977], para. 665.

[27] *Holloway* v. *Arthur Andersen & Co.*, 566 F. 2d 659, 661 [9th Cir. 1977], para. 665.

was meant to be liberally interpreted.[28] Concerning the meaning of the term "sex," Judge Grady claimed that "sex" should not be "a cut-and-dried matter of chromosomes" and it should be interpreted to include sexual identity.[29] Moreover, the judge questioned the existence of a settled definition of the term "sex" in the medical community.[30] Apart from seeing "sex" from a biological approach, it should also be understood from a psychological perspective that considers one's own self-perception and social perception of the specific individual.[31] Judge Grady addressed the importance of gender presentation in everyday life since he found it difficult to tell the difference between the plaintiff and an "ordinary" (i.e. cisgender) woman. The plaintiff's postoperative status was also stressed by the Court because this allowed her to function in their view fully as a woman.[32] Unlike *Holloway*, Judge Grady did not make reference to dictionary definitions regarding the term "sex." What the judge stressed was the broad interpretation of "sex." Under this approach, the judge held that the term "sex" literally and scientifically applies to transgender individuals.[33] The judge further suggested an alternative fallback: "if on appeal Title VII is held not to apply to transsexuals, then plaintiff should have a ruling on her alternative position that she is a female."[34] The judge also found the plaintiff's postoperative legal status as a female.

However, the Seventh Circuit Court of Appeals reversed the District Court decision by applying the ordinary, common meaning of the statute. Similar to *Holloway*, the Court adopted a traditional and narrow approach in interpreting the term "sex" and stressed the significance of complying with the congressional intent.[35] Due to a limited legislative history that can explain the inclusion of the category of sex, the Court therefore held that Congress had never considered nor intended that this 1964 legislation could apply to anything other than the traditional concept of sex.[36] Concurring with the Ninth Circuit in *Holloway*, the Court stated that "if the term 'sex' as it is used in Title VII is to mean more than biological male or biological female, the new definition must come from Congress" and that Title VII could not protect transgender individuals.[37] Moreover, since Judge Grady's reasoning stressed that Eastern did not want "[a] *transsexual* in the cockpit," this Court

---

[28] *Holloway* v. *Arthur Andersen & Co.*, 566 F. 2d 659, 661 [9th Cir. 1977], para. 665.

[29] *Holloway* v. *Arthur Andersen & Co.*, 566 F. 2d 659, 661 [9th Cir. 1977], para. 824.

[30] *Holloway* v. *Arthur Andersen & Co.*, 566 F. 2d 659, 661 [9th Cir. 1977], para. 824.

[31] *Holloway* v. *Arthur Andersen & Co.*, 566 F. 2d 659, 661 [9th Cir. 1977], para. 823.

[32] *Holloway* v. *Arthur Andersen & Co.*, 566 F. 2d 659, 661 [9th Cir. 1977], para. 823.

[33] *Holloway* v. *Arthur Andersen & Co.*, 566 F. 2d 659, 661 [9th Cir. 1977], para. 825.

[34] *Holloway* v. *Arthur Andersen & Co.*, 566 F. 2d 659, 661 [9th Cir. 1977], para. 839.

[35] *Ulane* v. *Eastern Airlines, Inc.*, 742 F 2d 1081 [7th Cir. 1984], para. 1086.

[36] *Ulane* v. *Eastern Airlines, Inc.*, 742 F 2d 1081 [7th Cir. 1984], para. 1086.

[37] *Ulane* v. *Eastern Airlines, Inc.*, 742 F 2d 1081 [7th Cir. 1984], para. 1087.

therefore concluded that Ulane was discriminated against by Eastern Airlines as a transgender person but not as a female and thereby, not being a protected class under the Act.[38]

2.2.2 Expanding the Terms "Because of . . . Sex" and Applying Sex-Stereotyping Theory to Title VII

Moving on from the two cases in Section 2.2.1, which ruled that transgender individuals failed to establish a valid case under Title VII, the following two cases decided that transgender plaintiffs can be protected under Title VII "discriminat[ion] . . . because of . . . sex" in two ways: (1) the plaintiff was discriminated against by their employer because of gender nonconformity; and (2) the plaintiff was discriminated against by their employer simply because of transgender status or intention to undergo gender confirmation surgery.

Smith v. City of Salem Ohio [2004]

In *Smith* v. *City of Salem Ohio*, Jimmie L. Smith was employed by the City of Salem as a lieutenant in its fire department.[39] The plaintiff is a transgender woman and was diagnosed with gender identity disorder (GID; a term that has been used in the case). After being diagnosed with GID, Smith began "expressing a more feminine appearance on a full-time basis," which then caused the plaintiff's coworkers to begin commenting that "[her] appearance and mannerisms were not 'masculine enough.'"[40] In response to those comments, Smith notified her immediate supervisor, defendant Thomas Eastek, about her GID diagnosis and the likelihood that she would eventually complete physical transformation from male to female with the hope that "Eastek could address Smith's co-workers' comments and inquiries."[41] Soon after the conversation, Eastek informed Walter Greenamyer, chief of the fire department, about Smith's behavior and her GID. Greenamyer had a meeting with the law director for the City of Salem, "with the intention of using Smith's transsexualism and its manifestations as a basis for terminating his employment."[42] They came up with an idea to "require Smith to undergo three separate psychological evaluations with physicians of the City's choosing."[43] They hoped that Smith would either resign or refuse to comply, which would then cause her to be terminated.

---

[38] *Ulane* v. *Eastern Airlines, Inc.*, 742 F 2d 1081 [7th Cir. 1984], para. 1087.
[39] *Smith* v. *City of Salem Ohio*, 369 F.3d 912 [6th Cir. 2004].
[40] *Smith* v. *City of Salem Ohio*, No. 4:02CV1405 [District Court, 2003], para. 1.
[41] *Smith* v. *City of Salem Ohio*, 369 F.3d 912 [6th Cir. 2004], para. 915.
[42] *Smith* v. *City of Salem Ohio*, 369 F.3d 912 [6th Cir. 2004], para. 915.
[43] *Smith* v. *City of Salem Ohio*, 369 F.3d 912 [6th Cir. 2004], para. 915.

Consequently, Smith filed a complaint against the City and various City officials under Title VII, claiming that the employee was discriminated against on the basis of sex.[44]

The case was first rejected by the District Court on the grounds that Title VII protection should not be applied to transgender individuals.[45] Before the *Smith* case, a groundbreaking judgment of *Price Waterhouse* v. *Hopkins* [1989] was delivered, which expanded the interpretation of the term "because of . . . sex." For both the District Court and the Supreme Court, it was unlawful for employers to discriminate against the plaintiff Ann Hopkins because she failed to act femininely. The Supreme Court held that discrimination because of "sex" includes gender discrimination: "[an] employer who acts on basis of belief that woman cannot be aggressive, or that she must not be, has acted on basis of gender for Title VII purposes."[46] The Supreme Court quoted that "[i]n forbidding employers to discriminate against individuals because of their sex, Congress intended to strike at the entire spectrum of disparate treatment of men and women resulting from sex stereotypes."[47] This case brought in another perspective of understanding the term "sex," for sex stereotyping (not just biological sex) should also be included under Title VII. Despite the broader *Price Waterhouse* approach in interpreting the term "because of . . . sex," the trial court of Smith held that even if the plaintiff had stated a claim of sex stereotyping, she still failed to demonstrate that [she] suffered an adverse employment action and that [she] failed to state a claim based on the deprivation of a constitutional or federal statutory right.[48] On appeal, the Sixth Circuit reversed the District Court's decision and applied the *Price Waterhouse* approach to reach the decision that transgender employees should be a member of a protected group under Title VII. The Court maintained that " discrimination against a plaintiff who is a transsexual – and therefore fails to act like and/or identify with the gender norms associated with his or her sex – is no different from the discrimination directed against Ann Hopkins in *Price Waterhouse*, who, in sex-stereotypical terms, did not act like a woman."[49] This shows that transgender individuals should be protected by the Act, for there is no difference between discrimination against a cisgender woman because she did not act in a feminine way and discrimination against a transgender woman because the employee did not perform in a masculine

---

[44] *Smith* v. *City of Salem Ohio*, 369 F.3d 912 [6th Cir. 2004], para. 915.

[45] *Smith* v. *City of Salem Ohio*, No. 4:02CV1405 [District Court, 2003].

[46] *Price Waterhouse* v. *Hopkins*, 490 US 228 [Supreme Court. 1989], p. 7.

[47] *Price Waterhouse* v. *Hopkins*, 490 US 228 [Supreme Court. 1989], p. 32 (quoting *Los Angeles Dept. of Water and Power* v. *Manhart*, 435 US 702, 707, n.13 [1978]).

[48] *Smith* v. *City of Salem Ohio*, No. 4:02CV1405 [District Court, 2003].

[49] *Smith* v. *City of Salem Ohio*, 369 F.3d 912 [6th Cir. 2004], para. 919.

way. More importantly, the Court stressed that a label, such as "transsexual," should not bar a person from being protected from the Act. The plaintiff should be protected both because of her gender nonconforming conduct and because of her identification as a transgender person.[50]

Schroer v. Billington [2008]

In *Schroer* v. *Billington*, the plaintiff, Diane Schroer, filed a complaint asserting that her employment was declined by the Librarian of Congress because of her transgender status, which should make her a member of the protected class under Title VII.[51] The plaintiff was offered a job as a specialist in terrorism and international crime with the Congressional Research Service (CRS) at the Library of Congress and received the highest interview score.[52] When the plaintiff, who was assigned male at birth, applied for this job, she had already been diagnosed with GID and had the intention to transition.[53] When the plaintiff notified Charlotte Preece, the Assistant Director for Foreign Affairs, Defense and Trade of CRS, about her plan to transition. Preece was shocked and commented that "everyone would know that [Schroer] had transitioned from male to female because only a man could have her military experiences."[54] In the end, Schroer's job offer was rescinded.

The District Court ruled in favor of the plaintiff by holding that several of the Library's stated reasons for revoking the plaintiff's job offer were pretext[s] for discrimination and that "the Library's conduct, whether viewed as sex stereo-typing or as discrimination literally 'because of sex,' violated Title VII."[55] The Court cited *Price Waterhouse* to support the point that the Library's decision about not hiring Schroer was sex discrimination based on her failure to conform to sex stereotypes.[56] It was clear to the Court that the Library's hiring decision was influenced by sex stereotypes since the person who made the decision, Preece, admitted that "when she viewed the photographs of Schroer in trad-itionally feminine attire, with a feminine hairstyle and makeup, she saw a man in women's clothing."[57] In addition, Preece found it difficult to understand Schroer's decision to transition, since she viewed the plaintiff not just as an

---

[50] *Smith* v. *City of Salem Ohio*, 369 F.3d 912 [6th Cir. 2004], para. 918.
[51] *Schroer* v. *Billington*, 577 F. Supp. 2d 293 [District Court, 2008].
[52] *Schroer* v. *Billington*, 577 F. Supp. 2d 293 [District Court, 2008].
[53] *Schroer* v. *Billington*, 577 F. Supp. 2d 293 [District Court, 2008].
[54] *Schroer* v. *Billington*, 577 F. Supp. 2d 293 [District Court, 2008], para. 298.
[55] *Schroer* v. *Billington*, 577 F. Supp. 2d 293 [District Court, 2008], para. 299.
[56] *Schroer* v. *Billington*, 577 F. Supp. 2d 293 [District Court, 2008], para. 299.
[57] *Schroer* v. *Billington*, 577 F. Supp. 2d 293 [District Court, 2008], para. 305.

ordinary man, but as "a particularly masculine kind of man."[58] After reviewing the evidence, the judge declared that:

> Ultimately, I do not think that it matters for purposes of Title VII liability whether the Library withdrew its offer of employment because it perceived Schroer to be an insufficiently masculine man, an insufficiently feminine woman, or an inherently gender-nonconforming transsexual. One or more of Preece's comments could be parsed in each of these three ways. While I would therefore conclude that Schroer is entitled to judgment based on a *Price Waterhouse*-type claim for sex stereotyping, I also conclude that she is entitled to judgment based on the language of the statute itself.[59]

The Court refused to "draw sweeping conclusions about the reach of Title VII" in the *Schroer* case, such as downplaying the importance of biological sex under the interpretation of the term "sex" in law.[60] Instead, the judge concurred that "Title VII means what it says, and that the statute requires, not amendment, but only correct interpretation."[61] According to the Court, a "correct interpretation" of the statute can already protect transgender people from being discriminated against because of sex. The judge further held that the approach in *Ulane II* and *Holloway* was no longer a tenable approach to statutory construction.[62]

2.2.3 Recent Legal Development in Accepting "Transgender" as a Member of Protected Class under Title VII

Four years after the *Schroer* judgment, a decision was made by the Equal Employment Opportunity Commission (EEOC) in *Macy* v. *Holder* that has invited courts to consider other broader approaches when handling cases concerning transgender people's legal protection in employment discrimination cases under Title VII. This decision ruled that "claims of discrimination based on transgender status, also referred to as claims based on gender identity, are cognizable under Title VII's sex discrimination prohibition."[63] The decision further stated that "Title VII's prohibition on sex discrimination proscribes gender discrimination, and not just discrimination on the basis of biological sex."[64] The *Macy* decision suggested that the term "sex" "encompasses both sex – that is, the biological differences between men and women – and gender" under Title VII.[65] This ruling is crucial in the sense

---

[58] *Schroer* v. *Billington*, 577 F. Supp. 2d 293 [District Court, 2008], para. 305.

[59] *Schroer* v. *Billington*, 577 F. Supp. 2d 293 [District Court, 2008], paras. 305–306.

[60] *Schroer* v. *Billington*, 577 F. Supp. 2d 293 [District Court, 2008], para. 308.

[61] *Schroer* v. *Billington*, 577 F. Supp. 2d 293 [District Court, 2008], para. 308.

[62] *Schroer* v. *Billington*, 577 F. Supp. 2d 293 [District Court, 2008], para. 308.

[63] *Macy* v. *Holder*, No. 0120120821, 2012 WL 1435995 [E.E.O.C. Apr. 20, 2012].

[64] *Macy* v. *Holder*, No. 0120120821, 2012 WL 1435995 [E.E.O.C. Apr. 20, 2012], p. 6.

[65] *Macy* v. *Holder*, No. 0120120821, 2012 WL 1435995 [E.E.O.C. Apr. 20, 2012], p. 6.

that it allows the term "sex" to be interpreted in a broader sense and highly increases the chance for transgender plaintiffs to successfully establish a case under Title VII. Even though the EEOC ruling on *Macy* was still not strictly binding on courts, it did set a strong trend in court decisions, holding that transgender people themselves are protected from discrimination (Beyer et al., 2014).

In 2020, a landmark decision (6–3 opinion) on *Bostock* v. *Clayton County* was handed down by the Supreme Court, ruling that homosexual and transgender individuals are entitled to federal employment discrimination protection. Unlike the previous cases, which mainly concerned transgender individuals, this case includes both homosexual and transgender plaintiffs and ruled that Title VII prohibits employers from terminating one's employment because that person is homosexual or transgender.[66] Donald Zarda, who worked at Altitude Express in New York as a skydiving instructor, was fired by the company after he had mentioned his homosexuality. Aimee Stephens, who worked at R. G. & G. R. Harris Funeral Homes in Garden City, Michigan, was fired after she had been diagnosed with gender dysphoria and indicated her plan to live and work "full-time as a woman."[67] Quoting from the *Price Waterhouse* decision, Justice Gorsuch held that " Title VII's message is 'simple but momentous' ... The statute's message for our cases is equally simple and momentous: An individual's homosexuality or transgender status is not relevant to employment decisions. That's because it is impossible to discriminate against a person for being homosexual or transgender without discriminating against that individual based on sex."[68] The Court concluded that when an employer fired an employee because of the person's transgender status, the person's "sex plays an unmistakable and impermissible role in the discharge decision."[69] While interpreting the meaning of the term "sex," the Court took the employers' assumption that it refers to the biological distinctions between men and women. This, however, can only be treated as the starting point in interpreting the statute since the statute also needs to be construed as a whole: "because of ... sex" as the Court has explained, should be understood in its "ordinary meaning of 'because of ' is 'by reason of' or 'on account of.'"[70] Using this causation standard in interpreting the statute language, the but-for causation standard is

---

[66] *Bostock* v. *Clayton County*, Nos. 17–1618, 17–1623 and 18–107.
[67] *Bostock* v. *Clayton County*, Nos. 17–1618, 17–1623 and 18–107.
[68] *Bostock* v. *Clayton County*, Nos. 17–1618, 17–1623 and 18–107. Quoting from *Price Waterhouse* v. *Hopkins*, 490 U. S. 228, 239 [1989].
[69] *Bostock* v. *Clayton County*, Nos. 17–1618, 17–1623 and 18–107.
[70] *Bostock* v. *Clayton County*, Nos. 17–1618, 17–1623 and 18–107.

met if the employee is not homosexual/transgender, and the employee will not be fired. In a dissenting judgment, Justice Alito (joined by Justice Thomas), however, stated that the textualist approach that the Supreme Court adopted is "preposterous" because to date, there are still differences between discrimination because of "sex" and discrimination because of "sexual orientation" and "gender identity."[71] Quoting from Scalia, Justice Alito held that judges' duty in statutory interpretation is to "mean what they conveyed to reasonable people at the time they were written."[72] Given that it would be very unlikely that people in 1964 would have thought that discrimination because of sex meant discrimination on the basis of sexual orientation and gender identity, it is therefore absurd to make a decision that the literal meaning of the statute in 1964 can encompass a different interpretation in 2020.[73]

These cases show that there is a progressive trend in protecting transgender individuals under anti-discrimination law. However, this change in the law of Title VII in fact has been building for the past decade. The following legal analysis of cases that concerned the phrase "because of . . . sex" under Title VII investigates the historical development of the Title VII law back from 1977. Through understanding how the judges adopted a textualist approach and interpreted the phrase "because of . . . sex" in different ways, the following aims to find out how legal changes took place and how they can be reflected through the judges' reasoning and interpretation on the phrase "because of . . . sex."

2.3 Close Study of the Statutory Interpretation of the Term "Because of . . . Sex" in Title VII

When adopting the textualist approach to construe the statute, the courts mainly adopted two approaches to determine whether transgender plaintiffs can be protected by the Act: (1) interpret the term "sex" by using its "traditional (biological) meaning" and "ordinary meaning"; (2) expand the interpretation from a single word "sex" to the whole phrase "because of . . . sex" in Title VII. Different approaches led to different legal reasoning and in turn affected transgender people in distinct ways. The next subsection intends to have a close reading of the two approaches.

---

[71] *Bostock* v. *Clayton County*, Nos. 17–1618, 17–1623 and 18–107 (Dissenting), p. 3.

[72] *Bostock* v. *Clayton County*, Nos. 17–1618, 17–1623 and 18–107 (Dissenting), p. 3. Quoting from A. Scalia & B. Garner, *Reading Law: The Interpretation of Legal Texts* 16 [2012], p. 3.

[73] *Bostock* v. *Clayton County*, Nos. 17–1618, 17–1623 and 18–107 (Dissenting), p. 3.

2.3.1 Binary Biological Sex Approach

Holloway and *Ulane II* adopted the binary biological sex approach when interpreting the traditional and plain meaning of the term "sex" under Title VII. They both distinguished discrimination "because of sex" from discrimination because of what was understood at the time as a change of sex. Given that transgender individuals were discriminated against by the employers because of their intention to undergo gender transition, they were then not protected by the plain language of the statute. The meaning of the term "sex" is indexical in nature because it is dependent on the context in which it is used. The meaning of the term is not fixed but varies based on the social and linguistic context of the interpretation. For the court in *Holloway*, the term "sex" should be "given its traditional definition based on the anatomical characteristics which divide organisms into males and females" and should not be expanded beyond its traditional meaning.[74] "Plain meaning" indicates that the meaning of a provision is "clear" and "unambiguous" (Cunningham et al., 1993). When the courts used the "traditional meaning" to define the "plain meaning" of the term "sex," it seems that this meaning should be simple and unambiguous to the general public. The *Holloway* court quoted definitions of "sex" and "gender" from *Webster's Seventh New Collegiate Dictionary* as the sole reference in defining the "plain meaning" of the terms. Following *Holloway*, the court in *Ulane II* also stated that "words [in statute] should be given their ordinary, common meaning," and the term "sex" should only be given a narrow and traditional interpretation based on a binary understanding of biological sex.[75] The court also held that the section 2000e-2(a) means nothing more than its plain language of the statute implies.[76] Rather than quoting from dictionaries, the court in *Ulane II* quoted various academic articles that supported the idea that sex should be defined by biological factors, such as chromosomes, internal and external genitalia, hormones, and gonads, and that chromosomal sex could not be changed.[77] Even though both courts stated that the statute language should be interpreted in its "plain" and "ordinary meaning," judges in the two cases consulted different sources when arriving at the meaning of the word "sex." The process of reaching such "plain" and "ordinary meaning" could vary across different judges, and, one may add, across different ordinary language users. The courts' usage of different sources to define the meaning of "sex" demonstrates the indexical nature of the term and how its meaning can vary depending on the sources consulted by the interpreters.

---

[74] *Holloway* v. *Arthur Andersen & Co.*, 566 F. 2d 659, 661 [9th Cir. 1977], para. 661.
[75] *Ulane II* [1984], para. 10.   [76] Ibid.   [77] Ibid., para. 6.

Criticisms have been made on how courts often seem to uncritically adopt the binary biological sex approach in reaching the "traditional meaning" and "plain meaning" of sex. For example, there is a tendency for courts to formulaically recite arguments, such as "sex discrimination laws were not intended to protect transgender people and the 'plain' or 'traditional' meaning of the term 'sex' refers only to a person's biological identity as male or female, not to change of sex" (Broadus, 2006, p. 95). When reaching such decision, one observation is that some courts only carried out limited analysis of whether and how sex discrimination statutes could be or should be applied to transgender people (Broadus, 2006). Transgender people's sex or other discrimination claims were sometimes dismissed out of hand by the courts with very little rational analysis of the law (Currah & Minterm, 2000). Courts that rejected transgender protection under the discrimination law seems to consider only selected sources that favor a binary understanding of biological sex.

2.3.2 Searching for the "Plain Meaning" of "Sex"

Courts tend to view the meaning of the term "sex" as unambiguous given that the "traditional meaning" of it seems to pop up in people's mind immediately. This raises a further problem regarding word definition, namely the difficulty of accessing and justifying people's common-sense knowledge. Throughout the judgments in *Holloway* and *Ulane II*, the "traditional concept of sex" seemed to be obvious and unproblematic to the courts. For the two courts, it was indisputable that the plain meaning of the word "sex" should be should be a binary understanding of "biological sex" and that there was no room for other interpretation. Fish (1987) explains:

> A meaning that seems to leap off the page, propelled by its own self-sufficiency, is a meaning that flows from interpretive assumptions so deeply embedded that they have become invisible (p. 403).

Feldman (2000) further adds that "a plain meaning seems to jump off a page only if we uncritically accept certain assumptions or prejudices that seem to ground the supposedly plain meaning" (p. 909). Further to this point, Feldman (1996) proposes that even when one appears to grasp the meaning of the text immediately without consciously thinking about its meaning, "that immediate grasp is possible only because the individual is situated within a horizon constituted by traditions and prejudices" (p. 179). When the courts claimed that the statute should be given its plain meaning or their ordinary, common meaning, it is possible that they were in fact interpreting the seemingly "plain" or "common" meaning by merely their intuitive responses to the word "sex." In addition, the notion of having a truly "plain" and fixed meaning of a word in statutory interpretation is worth pondering. Whether the word "sex" means its "traditional" or "biological" meaning or a broader meaning that can encompass a more nuanced understanding of biology and an understanding beyond biology depends on how the judges selected the best suited meaning from the indexical field, which in turn can also reflect judges' ideological understanding of gender (Eckert, 2008; Calder, 2021). The *Holloway* judgment was served as a precedent for the court in *Ulane II* and had guided the court to reach the "plain meaning" of the term "sex." This shows that precedents can play a significant role in how construals (in this case judges) build connection between sign-vehicles and objects.

Instead of representing the objective truth of words, plain meaning normally varies among different people. This could be demonstrated in Supreme Court cases observed by Solan where all nine Justices agreed that the meaning of a provision was "plain," but split five to four over what that provision actually meant (Cunningham et al., 1993). In other words, even if people agree that the word should be given its "plain meaning," it is still difficult for them to reach a unanimous decision on what the "plain meaning" should be. As mentioned in Section 1, Eskridge (1994) proposes the term "dynamic interpretation" for it is almost impossible to claim universal objectivity in the language of statute. Every interpreter has their own interpretation and each way the person reads the simple texts are influenced by one's context (Eskridge, 1994). Because people often bring in different knowledge, experience, and backgrounds during interpretation, it is almost impossible for a perfectly "plain" meaning to be reached. When judges were interpreting the "plain meaning" of the statute, it could be possible that their backgrounds and previous experiences had also been integrated into the statutory interpretation. This is to say that "an interpreter's ideology includes not just her specific beliefs about an issue, but also the broader web of interconnected ideas and biases that condition the way she looks at an issue, the bases for her pre-understanding" in cultural and political aspects (Eskridge, 1994, p. 66). Hence, it is argued that it is difficult to have truly "plain" meaning in statutory interpretation given that every interpretation is largely and even inescapably affected by the judge's previous experience, beliefs, and conceptions. It is therefore important for us to investigate the validity of treating the binary understanding of biological sex as the instinctive and objective "plain" meaning of sex and to consider other possibilities of understanding the term "sex." Reference can be made to Judge Grady's statement in *Ulane I*, which stated that "sex" should not be "a cut-and-dried matter of chromosomes."[78] This statement reminds us of the complexity of the notion of "sex" and the importance of exploring other than a reductive biological understanding.

2.3.3 Textualisms: Different Textualist Approaches in Interpreting "Because of . . . Sex"

The textualist approach that was covered in Section 1 usually relies on the plain meaning of the statute and is understood as relatively "conservative." Textualists stressed that "the statutory text alone has survived the constitutionally prescribed process of bicameralism and presentment" and that "when a statute is clear in context, purposivist judges disrespect the legislative process by relying upon unenacted legislative history" (Manning, 2006, p. 73). They believe that it is not feasible for judges to accurately infer what Congress would have "intended" if they are presented with a "perceived mismatch between the statutory text and its apparent purpose" (Manning, 2006, pp. 74–75). The cases discussed generally concern the "plain" and "ordinary meaning" of "because of . . . sex." However, even when the same textualist approach has been used, different courts reached different decisions by adopting different approaches in construing the meaning of the statute. When judges in *Holloway* and *Ulane II* focused on the "plain" and "ordinary meaning" of mainly the term "sex," it tended to lead to a more "conservative" interpretation that emphasized the biological sex, causing transgender individuals to be excluded from the protected category under Title VII.

In addition to the decisions on *Holloway* and *Ulane II*, the same issue regarding categorization and binary gender identities could also be found in judgments that were in favor of the transgender plaintiffs, namely the dissenting judgment in *Holloway* and the district court judgment in *Ulane I*. People tend to find it difficult to think outside the category of sex and the heterosexual frame (Davies, 1997, p. 33). In the dissenting judgment in *Holloway* that seems to favor the transgender plaintiff, Judge Goodwin still stressed the binary gender distinction by classifying the plaintiff as a (cisgender) woman rather than a transgender person. From Judge Goodwin's perspective, it would be possible for the plaintiff to state a claim under the discrimination act because after her gender confirmation surgery, the transgender plaintiff could then be classified into the victim class as a female. For Judge Goodwin, even though the plaintiff was understood as a transgender person, the transgender status was not sufficient for her to be a specific member for protection. It is important for the transgender plaintiff to undergo gender confirmation surgery and to seek a legal

---

[78] *Ulane I* [1983], Para. 824.

position as a female person. This could allow her to fit the binary gender distinction that law maintains and make her comprehensible under the law. The judge also suggested that the plaintiff amend her pleading to conform to the evidence that she was discharged for transitioning instead of as a person who would like to undergo gender confirmation surgery.[79] The law's binary gender distinction left the transgender plaintiff unprotected as a transgender person under Title VII. Transgender plaintiffs who do not have the intention to undergo gender confirmation surgery or to be categorized as either male or female will then face difficulties in seeking protection under Title VII.

The same issue could be found in the District Court *Ulane I* judgment led by Judge Grady, which went in favor of the transgender plaintiff. Judge Grady still maintained the distinction between transgender and male or female. Sharpe (2002) criticizes this judgment for locating transgender both within and outside the dyad of male or female distinction (p. 144). The Seventh Circuit found ambiguity in the district court judgment by noting that the trial judge originally found that Eastern had discriminated against Ulane as a transgender person but had subsequently modified his findings to hold that Ulane was discriminated against as both a female and a transgender person (Sharpe, 2002, p. 144). This in fact suggested that the transgender plaintiff had to be identified as both transgender and female but not simply as a transgender person. Similar to the dissenting judgment in *Holloway*, merely being a transgender person failed to make the plaintiff a protected class under Title VII. The judgment was criticized for enforcing an artificial distinction between male/female and transgender individuals (Green, 1985). The importance of undergoing gender confirmation surgery was also underscored by Judge Grady, for Ulane's successful postoperative status made her a "true transsexual," able to successfully live as a woman.[80] This in fact limited the protected categories in the judgment to only those who can "demonstrate a successful postoperative course."[81]

On the other hand, another textualist approach that construes the whole term "because of ... sex" (the approach that has been adopted by the courts in *Smith*, *Schroer*, and *Bostock*) suggested a more "progressive" direction in interpreting the statute, which can allow transgender individuals to be protected by the Act. The three courts followed the *Price Waterhouse* decision, which ruled that "sex" could be expanded beyond the traditional concept of "biological sex" and could include gender stereotypes, suggesting a dynamic interpretation approach. The court could also go beyond the original intent of Congress to protect groups that Congress might not have envisaged. Statutory interpretation should be

---

[79] Ibid., para. 665.
[80] *Ulane v. Eastern Airlines, Inc.*, 581 F. Supp. 821 [DDC, 1983], para. 827.   [81] Ibid.

multifaceted and dynamic, "rather than single-faceted and static" (Eskridge, 1994, p. 49). *Price Waterhouse* and cases that followed, including *Smith, Schroer* and *Bostock*, illustrate how courts can move substantially in interpreting a particular statute, indicating an intertextual approach that relies on precedent (*Price Waterhouse*) that is additional to the immediate text itself. This approach also focused on the plain language and the correct interpretation of the whole term "because of . . . sex" rather than merely the word "sex." Unlike the courts in *Holloway* and *Ulane II*, these courts were not particularly concerned about the scientific definition of the word "sex." The *Schroer* court rejected the search for a scientific understanding of "sex" and understood the term "because of . . . sex" as a whole, an approach that was shared by the court in *Smith*. Such an approach provided the courts with a way of avoiding the need to respond to the scientific definition of sex by building a relationship between sex stereotyping and sex discrimination (Weiss, 2008). One possible reason behind such an approach is that the courts might be aware of the complexities and potentially narrowness of the word "sex." If the courts decided to follow the plain meaning approach by only interpreting the word "sex," the decisions might be heading towards those in *Holloway* and *Ulane II*. To allow a more progressive decision on cases that concern transgender individuals in Title VII, instead of focusing on the "plain meaning" of the word "sex," the *Schroer* court underscored the "plain language" of the statute and stressed the "correct interpretation" of the statute was to interpret the term "because of . . . sex" as a whole.

There has been an assumption that textualism is associated with a "conservative" legal movement while purposivism is linked to "progressive" outcome (Grove, 2020). Another perspective, however, can be brought to the understanding of textualism, for the same court in *Bostock* can display two textualism approaches. As Grove (2020) argues, the question is which textualism should be used by the court. In *Bostock*, there seems to be two different textualist approaches leading to different interpretation of the term "because of . . . sex." The first is the more formalistic textualist approach that "instructs interpreters to carefully parse the statutory language, focusing on semantic context," while another is the more flexible textualist approach that "permits interpreters to make sense of the text by considering policy and social context as well as practical consequences" (Grove, 2020, p. 279). The majority opinion in *Bostock* represents the formalistic textualist approach for Justice Gorsuch, himself self-proclaiming as textualist, "carefully parsed the statutory language" of Title VII and ruled that the "plain meaning" of "because of . . . sex" meant that "sex" should be a "but-for cause" of the employer's decision (Gorsuch, 2019). The term had to be understood as a whole and all decisions that are made on the basis of sex should be considered as part of the "plain meaning" of the statute. Such formalistic textualistic approach allows the court to reach a more progressive legal decision. The dissenting judgment in *Bostock* adopted the flexible textualist approach when Justice Alito argued that rather than purely relying on the statutory language, the importance of learning how the public would have understood the meaning of "sex" in the context of 1964 should be emphasised. Instead of only conforming to the literal meaning of the statute, this flexible textualist approach considers the social and policy context and the ordinary people's views in 1964 as well. Joining the dissenting judgment, Justice Kavanaugh also argued that the majority decision was improperly "literal" in its understanding of Title VII and that it led to absurdity doctrine.[82] However, such an "absurdity" of expanding "because of . . . sex" to include transgender individuals was understood in the historical context of 1964. The problem of this flexible textualist approach, as Justice Gorsuch wrote, is that it has placed the focus of the case on "expected public meaning," which could be seen as highly similar to purposivism that stresses the congressional intent or expectations (see also Grove, 2020). The flexible approach that has been exemplified in the dissenting judgment, hence, seems to have blurred the boundary between textualism and purposivism and suggested a rather fixed understanding of the term "sex," for its understanding needed to be framed in the past and in an imaginative form.

2.4 Conclusion

As the analysis shows, textualism does not necessarily lead to a rather "conservative" legal decision. The key is which textualist approach the court is using and how the court interprets the term "because of . . . sex." There are mainly two ways of interpreting the statute: (1) mainly interpreting the term "sex" and using a binary biological sex approach to define its meaning and reject the inclusion of transgender plaintiffs under the law; (2) interpreting the whole term "because of . . . sex" and ruling that a broader and more inclusive approach should be applied to cover all discriminatory decisions that are made on the basis of sex. For the first approach, it is obvious that the courts limited the understanding of "sex" to a binary understanding of biological factors and refused to acknowledge the legal status of transgender plaintiffs under Title VII. Transgender individuals, in this case, have been characterized as falling outside of the binary gender distinction. For the second approach, the courts allowed a broader approach that allows transgender plaintiffs to be protected by the Act. However, the discussion of whether the term "sex" should or should not be purely defined by a binary understanding of biological sex has not been initiated

---

[82] *See Bostock* v. *Clayton County*, Nos. 17–1618, 17–1623 and 18–107 (Kavanaugh, J., dissenting).

by the courts. For example, the *Schroer* court refused to downplay the importance of biological sex under the interpretation of the term "sex" in law. It seems that the courts still treat the binary biological sex approach as an important indicator when deciding the meaning of "sex." To adopt this "plain language of the whole term" approach, it can allow transgender plaintiffs to be protected by the Act without having the need to argue for the latest and "ordinary" understanding of "sex." Such an approach, despite its attempt in covering transgender plaintiffs, still fails to challenge the traditional and biological understanding of the term "sex." The next section will further enrich the discussion of the role of biology in defining one's sex and the ordinary heterosexist meaning of terms such as "man" and "woman" by looking at transgender identities in the context of marriage in common law jurisdictions. It aims to present how under the common law system, the UK court had first established a precedent in adopting a narrow and "biological" understanding of sex in transgender case and how such precedent has affected the later transgender cases in both the United Kingdom and Hong Kong (HKSAR).

3 Statutory Interpretations of "Man" and "Woman" in Marriage Law

3.1 Introduction

Section 2 illustrates how the binary gender distinction has been stressed by the law in antidiscrimination law. Such a binary distinction is also found to be maintained in marriage law for marriage has long been understood as a relationship between a (cisgender) man and a (cisgender) woman. One relatable reference can be drawn from the registrar's statement at the opening of a civil marriage ceremony: "Marriage according to the law of this country is the union of one man with one woman, voluntarily entered into for life, to the exclusion of all others" (see Hutton, 2019b, p. 64). The composition of "one man" and "one woman" has been commonly accepted, and sometimes treated unquestionably, as one of the essential natures of marriage. In *Notes and Queries in Anthropology*, marriage was defined as "a union between a man and a woman such that the children born to the woman are recognized as legitimate offspring of both parents" ([RAI], 1951, pp. 70–71). An older reference point of marriage can be drawn from the *Book of Common Prayer* (1662), which states that marriage is "an honorable estate, instituted of God in the time of man's innocence, signifying unto us the mystical union that is betwixt Christ and his Church" (see Bannet 1997). When making reference to "the time of man's innocence," this definition shows "an underlying 'natural law' theory of marriage: it is the sacred exchange of vows between a man and a woman before

God that constitutes the marriage contract" (Hutton, 2019b, p. 62). The emphasis on the union of a (cisgender) man and a (cisgender) woman can also be found in the common law definition of marriage. In the case of *Hyde* v. *Hyde & Woodmansee*,[83] a legal definition of marriage was provided by the court and marriage as understood in Christendom is "the voluntary union for life of one man and one woman, to the exclusion of all others." The phrase "one man and one woman" became the legal framing of marriage and has established its authoritative status in common law discourse (Hutton, 2019b). However, it is worth noting that despite the existence of a seemingly entrenched definition of "marriage," there are by far no statutory definitions of the terms "man" and "woman." This has put the onus on judges, especially those who needed to decide whether transgender people can marry in their affirmed sex, to interpret these terms. Defining the terms "man" and "woman" in marriage law can have significant impact on transgender people's legal rights for such a definition can affect whether the two people can receive recognition of their status from society as well as relevant rights and interests from the law.

Marriage has been chosen as the focus of this section because it involves the notions of authenticity and control. The notion of authenticity has been bought up to define what a moral agent is (Taylor, 1989). In law, it is important for one to exercise its authenticity with a self-controlling attitude in which the ultimate end is the exercise of discipline and of control over one's impulses (Ferrara, 1993). The idea of law is understood as a form of social contract in that the pursuit of self should be constrained by the benefits of sociality, conformity, and compromise (Hutton, 2019a). Law was seen as "a scheme of social control" (Willis, 1926, p. 204) and "the enterprise of subjecting human conduct to the governance of rules" (Fuller, 1967 p. 106). Instead of seeing marriage as a mere sacred contract, in *Lindo* v. *Belisario*,[84] Sir William Scott explained that marriage "is a contract according to the law of nature, antecedent to civil institution, which may take place to all intents and purposes, wherever two persons of different sexes engage, by mutual contracts, to live together." To enter such legal and social contract, two individuals need to be legally categorized as "two persons of different sexes" and fulfill the criteria of consummating a marriage. This section first concerns UK marriage cases that concern the notion of consummation and the definitions of "man" and "woman." The central argument of the UK marriage cases in *Corbett* v. *Corbett* (1971) and *Bellinger* v. *Bellinger* (2002), (2003) was whether a transgender woman who has undergone gender confirmation surgery can be categorized as a "woman." In response

---

[83] *Hyde* v. *Hyde and Woodmansee* [1866] LR 1 P & D 130, p. 130.
[84] *Lindo* v. *Belisario* [1795] C. R. 216., p. 374.

to the decisions in these two cases, *Goodwin* v. *United Kingdom* (2002) came to address how English law failed to give marriage rights to transgender persons who have undergone gender confirmation surgery. After discussing the UK marriage cases, this section then brings in a case study from Hong Kong, focusing on transgender positioning in Hong Kong's marriage cases.

3.2 Transgender People in UK Marriage Cases (1971–2003)

3.2.1 Cases Analysis

Corbett v. *Corbett* (1971)

Being regarded as one of the most influential common law cases that concern whether a transgender person can be legally categorized and therefore, married in his/her affirmed sex, *Corbett* v. *Corbett*[85] calls into question the fundamental notions of the definitions of "man" and "woman" as well as the "authentic" sexual organ, together with its ability to consummate a marriage. The petitioner, Arthur Cameron Corbett, sought a declaration that the marriage between him and the respondent, April Ashley, was void, since the respondent at the time of the marriage was a person of male sex.[86] In addition, the petitioner claimed that the marriage should be declared as void since it was never consummated due to the incapacity or wilful refusal of the respondent to do so.[87] Concerning the act of "consummation," Dr. Lushington argued in the case of *D*. v. *A*.[88] that it required an "ordinary and (a) complete intercourse." In *D*. v. *A*., as mentioned in *Corbett*, the wife had no uterus and her vagina was undeveloped, and therefore "only a very partial insertion of the penis" was possible.[89] Because of the incapacity for an "ordinary and (a) complete intercourse" to take place, the marriage was annulled. One of the central questions in *Corbett* lies in whether a transgender woman who has undergone gender confirmation surgery can be defined as a woman in marriage law and to have a marriage consummated. According to the judge Ormrod J., who is also a medical practitioner, the true sex of the respondent should mainly decide the validity of the marriage.[90] As stated by the judge, *Corbett was* "the first occasion on which a court in England has been called upon to decide the sex of an individual" and he ruled that in the context of marriage, the criteria of defining a "woman" must be biological:[91]

---

[85] *Corbett* v. *Corbett* [1971] P 83 (HL).   [86] *Corbett* v. *Corbett* [1971] P 83 (HL), p. 84.
[87] *Corbett* v. *Corbett* [1971] P 83 (HL), p. 85.
[88] *D*. v. *A*., 1 Rob. Eccl. Rep. 279 [1845], p. 298.
[89] *D*. v. *A*., 1 Rob. Eccl. Rep. 279 [1845], p. 285.   [90] *Corbett* v. *Corbett* [1971] P 83 (HL), p. 89.
[91] *Corbett* v. *Corbett* [1971] P 83 (HL), p. 106.

> [F]or even the most extreme degree of transsexualism in a male or the most severe hormonal imbalance which can exist in a person with male chromosomes, male gonads and male genitalia cannot reproduce a person who is naturally capable of performing the essential role of a woman in marriage.[92]

"Doctor's criteria" including chromosomal, gonadal, and genital were the major biological factors that the court concerned.[93] The congruence of these biologicalfactors was emphasized by the court, leading to the decision that "the respondent is not a woman for the purposes of marriage but is a biological male and has been so since birth."[94] According to the court, the gender confirmation surgery that the transgender person underwent would never turn her into a woman in the eyes of the law since "the respondent's operation ... cannot affect her true sex."[95] The court concluded that the respondent failed to perform the "essential role of a woman in marriage," which was to consummate the marriage "naturally."[96] For Ormrod, it was never possible for a person's true sex to be altered through any surgical intervention. According to the judge, "sex is clearly an essential determinant of the relationship called marriage because it is and always has been recognized as the union of man and woman."[97] April Ashley's gender confirmation surgery, from the court's perspective, will not turn her into a "woman" in the context of marriage, and the marriage between her and the petitioner should be declared as void. The authenticity of one's sex has been stressed by the court through emphasizing the notion of "true sex." It is worth noting that law, as explained by Ormrod at the opening of his post-*Corbett* lecture, was itself an "artefact," a "system of regulations which depends on precise definitions" (Ormrod, 1972, p. 78). Law was "obliged to classify its material into exclusive categories; it is therefore, a binary system designed to produce conclusions of the *Yes* or *No* type" (Ormrod, 1972, p. 78). The binary categorization and biological understanding of a person's sex that were suggested in *Corbett* have ever since set a fundamental and even limiting framework for the subsequent transgender cases in marriage law.

Bellinger v. Bellinger (2002)

Bellinger v. *Bellinger* is the first decision in Britain to revisit *Corbett* significantly (Hutton, 2019b). Similar to *Corbett*, the legal question in *Bellinger* was whether at the time of the marriage, Mrs Bellinger, a transgender woman assigned male at birth who had undergone gender confirmation surgery, was "female" within the meaning of section 1(c) of the Nullity of Marriage Act

---

[92] *Corbett* v. *Corbett* [1971] P 83 (HL), p. 106. [93] *Corbett* v. *Corbett* [1971] P 83 (HL), p. 106.
[94] *Corbett* v. *Corbett* [1971] P 83 (HL), p. 106. [95] *Corbett* v. *Corbett* [1971] P 83 (HL), p. 104.
[96] *Corbett* v. *Corbett* [1971] P 83 (HL), p. 106. [97] *Corbett* v. *Corbett* [1971] P 83 (HL), p. 105.

1971, re-enacted in section 11(c) of the Matrimonial Causes Act 1973, which stated that a marriage is void unless the parties are "respectively male and female."[98] When summarizing the background of the case, the *Corbett* criteria were adopted, treating them as a fundamental framework in deciding a person's sex[99]:

> At birth Mrs Bellinger was registered as male but there was ambiguity about her upbringing in childhood and it seems her mother had wanted her to be a girl and in fact dressed her as such. When she was 20 Mrs Bellinger married a woman. At that time, according to the *Corbett* criteria, Mrs Bellinger was undoubtedly male. Her chromosomes were XY, she had testicles and she had a penis. She certainly did not have a vagina, a uterus or ovaries. She and the woman she had married had a sexual relationship capable of producing a child.

The House of Lords in *Bellinger* followed *Corbett* and upheld the Court of Appeal decision of 2001. Before the House of Lords decision, there was a dissenting judgment in the Court of Appeal by the judge L. J. Thorpe. Justice Thorpe rejected the *Corbett* biological factors and physiological criteria since this restricted approach was believed not to be permissible in the light of scientific, medical, and social changes.[100] He was dubious about treating chromosomal factor as conclusive in the context of marriage since "it is an invisible feature of an individual, incapable of perception or registration other than by scientific test."[101]

While noting that the decision in *Corbett* had been criticized as "reductionistic" and that it was not followed by some of the overseas jurisdictions, for instance in Australia and New Zealand,[102] the House of Lords in *Bellinger* still affirmed *Corbett*'s approach. The court quoted extensively from *Corbett* and held that it was crucial to apply objective "biological" criteria to categorize a person's sex.[103] For the court, self-definition was not acceptable since "individuals cannot choose for themselves whether they wish to be known or treated as male or female."[104] Even though the court in *Bellinger* concurred with the judge J. Chisholm in Australian transgender marriage case *Re Kevin* that the words "male" and "female" were "not technical terms and that they must be given their ordinary, everyday meaning in the English language," the judge eventually arrived at a conclusion by holding that the words "male" and

---

[98] *Bellinger* v. *Bellinger* [2003] WL 1610368.
[99] *Bellinger* v. *Bellinger* [1999] High Court of Justice (Fam. Div), Case No. 69 of 1999, p. 2.
[100] *Bellinger* v. *Bellinger* [2002] Fam. 150, p. 188.
[101] *Bellinger* v. *Bellinger* [2002] Fam. 150, p. 191.
[102] *Bellinger* v. *Bellinger* [2003] WL 1610368, p. 3.
[103] *Bellinger* v. *Bellinger* [2003] WL 1610368, p. 5.
[104] *Bellinger* v. *Bellinger* [2003] WL 1610368, p. 5.

"female" should be understood in the context of United Kingdom and could not include transgender people who had undergone gender confirmation surgery.[105] Following *Corbett*, the court also held that a person's sex could not be changed and thereby, declining to give "a novel, extended meaning" to the words, which could include transgender people.[106] In response to the *Goodwin* judgment (discussed next), however, the court had no option but to make a declaration of incompatibility given that section 11(c) of the Matrimonial Causes Act 1973 was incompatible with Mrs. Bellinger's Convention rights. However, the court still held that the marriage in this case was invalid and that the ordinary meaning of "male" and "female" could not encompass postoperative transgender people. The United Kingdom thereafter enacted the Gender Recognition Act (2004).

Goodwin v. *United Kingdom* (2002)

On the notion of marriage, the European Court of Human Rights (ECHR) in the *Goodwin* held that it was a breach of the right to marry if a transgender person who had undergone gender confirmation surgery could only marry a person of opposite sex to the sex they were assigned at birth.[107] This decision was given after the *Bellinger* decision in the Court of Appeal. The decision finds that it is artificial to assert that transgender individuals who had undergone gender confirmation surgery have not been deprived of the right to marry as, according to law, they remain able to marry a person of the opposite sex to the sex they were assigned at birth. The applicant in this case identifies as a woman, is in a relationship with a man, and would only wish to marry a man. She has no possibility of doing so. In the court's view, she may therefore claim that the very essence of her right to marry has been infringed.[108] In terms of this case's reasoning, it is important to note that the ECHR in fact rejected *Corbett* since there had been "major social changes in the institution of marriage," which can be reflected by "the adoption of the Convention as well as dramatic changes brought about by developments in medicine and science in the field of transsexuality."[109] The court also could no longer accept the *Corbett* binary biological sex approach as dominant or decisive in determining a person's sex and the legal recognition of transgender people.[110] Moreover, the court took into account the acceptance of the conditions of gender identity disorder (GID; a term used at the time) by medical professions and health authorities within

---

[105] *Bellinger* v. *Bellinger* [2003] WL 1610368, p. 11.
[106] *Bellinger* v. *Bellinger* [2003] WL 1610368, p. 6.
[107] *Goodwin* v. *United Kingdom* [2002] 35 EHRR 18, para. 101.
[108] *Goodwin* v. *United Kingdom* [2002] 35 EHRR 18, para. 101.
[109] *Goodwin* v. *United Kingdom* [2002] 35 EHRR 18, para. 100.
[110] *Goodwin* v. *United Kingdom* [2002] 35 EHRR 18, para. 100.

Contracting States and the significance of surgical treatment including gender confirmation surgery.[111] After considering all thesematters, the ECHR therefore concluded that "the Court finds no justification for barring the transsexual from enjoying the right to marry under any circumstances."[112]

3.2.2 Legal Interpretation and Categorization of the Terms "Man" and "Woman" in UK Marriage Law (1971–2003)

The seemingly fixed understanding of the notions of sex and sexuality are produced through discourse (Foucault 1978; Butler 1999). Among these discourses, Foucault (1978) argues that legal discourse establishes reality, desires, sex, and uses its power to control and suppress different sexual and gender expressions. When analyzing how the judges in *Corbett* and *Bellinger* determined the meaning of "woman" in marriage law, it is found that the judges adopted the binary biological sex approach and ruled out other possibilities in viewing one's sex. They thereby established a "reality" of sex in law, which sometimes even resulted in "a fractured and incoherent notion of legal sex" (Hutton, 2019b, p. 118). The following discusses how the judges in *Corbett* and *Bellinger* stressed the importance of "true sex" through maintaining the binary biological sex approach and how the judges in *Bellinger* interpreted the ordinary meaning of the word "woman."

Binary Biological Sex Approach: The Upholding of "True Sex"

When defining the term "woman," the Judge J. Ormrod in *Corbett* mainly based his reasoning on the medical evidence, which involved "a unusually large number of doctors" to give evidence in the case, "amounting to no less than nine in all."[113] When explaining how a person's sex should be decided, Ormrod stated that:

> [T]he law should adopt in the first place, the first three of the doctors' criteria, i.e., the chromosomal, gonadal and genital tests, and if all three are congruent, determine the sex for the purpose of marriage accordingly, and ignore any operative intervention.[114]

Other than biological criteria, no other evidence nor criterion was considered. The judge also stressed the importance of authenticity in viewing one's sex, for sexual organs that involve surgical intervention should be treated as "artificial." In the judgment, Ormrod stated that April Ashley only possessed an "artificial

---

[111] *Goodwin* v. *United Kingdom* [2002] 35 EHRR 18, para. 100.
[112] *Goodwin* v. *United Kingdom* [2002] 35 EHRR 18, para. 103.
[113] *Corbett* v. *Corbett* [1971] P 83 (HL), para. 89.
[114] *Corbett* v. *Corbett* [1971] P 83 (HL), para. 106.

cavity."[115] In the *Medico-Legal Journal*, Ormrod (1972) also named the surgically constructed vagina as "a pseudo-vagina artificially constructed in a male" (p. 85). This binary biological sex approach, which emphasized the authenticity of a person's sex, has been criticized for abstracting a legal principle out of the medical evidence and failing to consider other possibilities of viewing one person's sex (Hutton, 2011). This binary biological sex approach was adopted by the *Bellinger* court and was treated as the main reasoning for defining the term "woman."

Some of the contents of biology were generally treated as a principle of normality of human sexuality that can hardly be questioned (Foucault, 1978). This can be reflected in both *Corbett* and *Bellinger* cases. However, Foucault (1978) questions the existence of the "truth" of sex and argues that the notion of "sex" is only an artificial unity which is used to group different elements together, for instance, anatomical elements, biological functions, and conduct. For him, there is an artificial binary relationship between the sexes, which stresses an artificial internal coherence among the notion of sex (Foucault, 1978, Butler, 1999). Vade (2004) adds to this argument by saying that "sex is gender pretending to be objective scientific truth" (p. 291). Butler (1998) also suggests that "the regulatory practices that generate coherent identities through the matrix of coherent gender norms" produce the idea that there might be a "truth" of sex (p. 24). There is also no underlying essence to one's gender performativity given that human beings do their gender though imitation and reiteration of others' gender performance (Butler, 1998). Performativity implies that the body "gains its meaning through a concrete and historically mediated expression in the world" (Butler, 1988, p. 521). The performativity of gender therefore suggests no ontological reasoning behind the construction of gender, and there is also no truth of sex. Thus, the courts' approach of treating biological sex as the "truth" of sex can be challenged, suggesting that those concepts can be artificial and can be a construction of social norms, law, and different forms of regulatory powers.

Finding the "Ordinary Meaning" of "Male" and "Female" in Marriage Law

As mentioned, *Bellinger* followed *Corbett* in adopting the binary biological sex approach when defining a person's sex. Even though the role of language was not investigated by the *Corbett* court, in the Court of Appeal, the judges in *Bellinger* did consider the ordinary meaning of those words as part of their

---

[115] *Corbett* v. *Corbett* [1971] P 83 (HL), para. 107.

reasoning.[116] For the court, the "single, clear meaning" of "male" and "female" as stated in the *Corbett* decision must be followed by the court.[117] The court also held that "a novel, extended meaning" of the words "male" and "female" would be resulted if Mrs. Bellinger, a transgender woman assigned male at birth, is recognized as female for the purposes of the act.[118] Agreeing with the Australian judges in *Re Kevin* that the words "male" and "female" need to be understood in their ordinary, everyday meanings in the English language, House of Lords came to a conclusion that the ordinary meaning of those words fail to include transgender people, even those who have had gender confirmation surgery in the context of the U.K ...[119] For the court, there was no evidence suggesting "that in contemporary usage in the country, on whichever date one might wish to select" that "these words can be taken to include post-operative transsexual persons."[120] Holding that an ordinary meaning in the English language must be given to the words "male" and "female," the definition of the word "male" from *New Shorter Oxford English Dictionary* (1983) stating that its "primary meaning when used as an adjective is 'of, pertaining to, or designating the sex which can beget offspring.'"[121] The court also highlighted the absence of "transexual persons" in the definition.[122]

Despite the fact that the Australian courts have differentiated transgender persons who have and have not undergone gender confirmation surgery by addressing "the contemporary usage of the word in Australia," the *Bellinger* court stated that such understanding is "absent from the ordinary meaning of the word "male" in the country."[123] The *Bellinger* court's reasonings suggest that the "ordinary meanings" of the words "man" and "woman," "male" and "female" are to be understood in a specific context, and it could vary across different countries. It further implies that the meanings of "man" and "woman" differ in both Australia and England. There is, however, no concrete evidence on justifying such differences. The *Corbett* case has set a precedent for the *Bellinger* courts and has produced "controlling images" of "woman" in marriage law. Such "controlling images" can be seen as some ideological representations of individuals which take part in reinforcing problematic stereotypes about minority groups (Hill-Collins, 1990). Such images also frame how marginalized groups get interpreted and understood, largely through the lens

---

[116] *Bellinger* v. *Bellinger* [2002] Fam. 150., p. 10.
[117] *Bellinger* v. *Bellinger* [2002] Fam. 150., p. 10.
[118] *Bellinger* v. *Bellinger* [2002] Fam. 150., p. 6.
[119] *Bellinger* v. *Bellinger* [2003] WL 1610368.
[120] *Bellinger* v. *Bellinger* [2003] WL 1610368, para. 62.
[121] *Bellinger* v. *Bellinger* [2003] WL 1610368, para. 62.
[122] *Bellinger* v. *Bellinger* [2003] WL 1610368, para. 62.
[123] *Bellinger* v. *Bellinger* [2003] WL 1610368, para. 62.

of the majority group (Calder, 2021). Through building an indexical link between the word "woman" and bodies that are biologically assigned female (as suggested by medical experts in *Corbett* and dictionary definitions in *Bellinger*), both courts are treating transgender women to be less than cisgender women or even non-women, rendering indexical patterns of the courts' only approved image of women (adopting the biology criteria) to be the "prescriptive benchmark" against which the transgender women are compared (Calder, 2021, p. 45). Under these circumstances, transgender women will only be excluded under the "ordinary meaning" approach that both courts have adopted. The following section intends to provide a case study on how transgender people are understood in Hong Kong, aiming to grapple with how the meanings of "man" and "woman" are to be situated in a specific context and whether gender possibilities can be allowed by law.

3.3 Transgender People in Hong Kong Marriage Law

3.3.1 Understanding "Transgender" in Hong Kong

The current form of legal system in Hong Kong is the common law system. In terms of the legal system, it is argued that there is a colonial time lag in Hong Kong's practices in drawing on the United Kingdom process of legislative reform and drafting (Hutton, 2014b). This colonial time lag can be reflected in Hong Kong's case *W v Registrar of Marriages* (2013 concerning the right of a transgender woman who has undergone gender confirmation surgery to marry in her affirmed sex which came more than ten years after the passage of Gender Recognition Act 2004 in the United Kingdom. The Hong Kong *W* judgment ruled that a transgender woman who has undergone gender confirmation surgery can be legally married in her affirmed sex. Thr Gender Recognition Act, however, is still not being implemented in Hong Kong. Hong Kong is seen as "an only partially modernized or semi- traditional Chinese society with its own distinct moral code and ethical attitudes" (Hutton, 2014b, p. 229–230). It has its own way of viewing and processing transgender-related topics that were once introduced and circulated in Western context, causing transgender people to be caught between the Chinese and Westernized understanding of transgender identities (see Tao, 2022). This further led to and even intensified the transphobia that transgender individuals can experience within the Hong Kong society and among the Hong Kong transgender community (Tao, 2022). In addition, Hong Kong has no laws against discrimination on the grounds of sexual orientation and gender identity, rendering transgender people's legal protection against discrimination questionable. As of 2022, transgender people are not covered by Hong Kong's "Sex Discrimination Ordinance" which only covers discrimination against an individual who is either a (cisgender) woman or a (cisgender) man but fails to address discrimination based on gender identity. This has further increased the possibilities for transgender individuals to experience difficulties in the workplace, such as problems regarding usage of washrooms, privacy issues, bullying and harassment and gender transition (Transgender Equality Hong Kong, 2021). This section will discuss to discuss the legal and social understanding of a person's sex in the context of Hong Kong and explore the futurity of having transgender rights being recognized in Hong Kong.

In Hong Kong, the space for discussing LGBT issues has long been known as relatively limited, with transgender issues be even more hidden in the past few decades (Emerton, 2006; Wan, 2020). According to a 2012 survey commissioned by Community Business, 77 per cent of the working population respondents said they did not know the meaning of the term "transgender" (Chow, 2013). Even though no full details on the size of the survey and the background of the respondents were provided, this survey can provide us with an introductory point to make sense of the society's seemingly limited understanding of transgender issues. In 2020, transgender organizations estimated that there could be around 18,000 transgender individuals in Hong Kong (Lin, 2020). However, this group is often underrepresented since Hong Kong society arguably lacks comprehensive understanding of the transgender community. It has been reported that transgender people are still facing different forms of discrimination in the workplace and in society (King, 2003). A survey reported that 76 percent of the transgender respondents had encountered different forms of rejection in social life which is mainly due to the public misunderstanding and stereotypes against transgender people in the society (Suen, Chan & Wong, 2021). In most cases, transgender people, especially those who have not undergone gender confirmation surgery, are still being treated by the law in their assigned sex as recorded on their birth certificate. In Hong Kong, gender confirmation surgery is a procedure that is fully subsidized by the government, alongside other gender transitional-related treatments. The person can only apply for a change of the sex marker on their Hong Kon permanent identity card when the person has completed the gender confirmation surgery. However, changing their sex on their birth certificate is still not possible in Hong Kong. As for those who have not undergone or completed the surgery, they will have to undergo psychiatric assessment and go through a period of "real life experience," a process where they live in the gender role different from the one they were assigned at birth, before they can seek for other medical help related to their Gender Dysphoria, such as hormone treatment. Their sex on their personal document will only be changed when the surgery is completed. In Hong Kong, public toilets represent a legal gray area, where a transgender person who uses gender-appropriate toilet but one which does not match their ID card may face police questioning or even a charge of loitering or disorderly conduct (Cheung 2016) while in the United Kingdom, transgender persons who are undergoing gender transition (irrespective of the involvement of surgical procedures), are fully supported in using all facilities (including toilets) in accordance with their gender. Thus, in Hong Kong, the completion of the gender confirmation surgery is of paramount importance in transgender people's legal and social positioning. It also plays a significant role in affecting how a transgender person can be categorized. The following addresses how transgender people are perceived in Hong Kong marriage law.

3.3.2 W. v. Registrar of Marriage *(2010), (2011), and (2013)*

The Hong Kong case *W v Registrar of Marriage* (2010), (2011), and (2013) is the Hong Kong Court of First Instance judgment that concerns a transgender individual's right to marry. This case was first decided by the High Court in 2010 and was then brought to the Court of Appeal in 2011. The challenge failed in both the High Court and the Court of Appeal. However, a landmark judgment was handed down in 2013 by Hong Kong's highest court, the Court of Final Appeal, ruling that the appeal was allowed and that Ms. W, a transgender woman assigned male at birth who had undergone gender confirmation surgery, was in law entitled to be included as "a woman" within the meaning of the Marriage Ordinance. This case has sparked off intensive discussion on transgender people's right in Hong Kong. An entire volume of the *Hong Kong Law Journal* (vol. 41) was published in 2011 to discuss law regarding transgender people in Hong Kong and the *W* case was the main focus of discussion (see Hutton 2011). Following that, there were also many forums and talks on the *W* case. When the case was first decided by the High Court, the judge Andrew Cheung J was aware of the different interpretations of the terms "man" and "woman" in Australia and the United Kingdom. Regarding such differences, he held that:

> the Australian courts have been able to say that in the English language as used in Australia, the words 'man' and 'woman' (and 'male' and 'female') include respectively a post-operative transsexual man and a post-operative transsexual woman. However, this is apparently not so in the United Kingdom.[124]

---

[124] *W*. v. *Registrar of Marriages* [2010] 6 HKC 359, para. 136.

As mentioned in the judgment, the terms "man" and "woman" were not defined by the Marriage Ordinance and the Matrimonial Causes Ordinance and that the matter was "left to the interpretation of the court."[125] Justice Cheung is also aware of the point that there is "very little evidence placed before the Court regarding the ordinary, everyday usage of the relevant words in this jurisdiction," as well as to "how the local usage and understanding differed from vase law in other jurisdictions."[126] When deciding the meaning of the words "man" and "woman" in the context of Hong Kong, the court stated that *Corbett* represented the state of Hong Kong law and that its "binary biological sex approach" should be adopted.[127] The court stressed the importance of procreation in marriage and reaffirmed that the ordinary meaning of the words "man" and "woman" should not include a transgender person who has undergone gender confirmation surgery. He further stated that:

> Whilst it is quite true that a sex reassignment surgery is colloquially referred to as a 'sex change operation' (變性手術), so far as the Court observes, the reference to 'sex change' (變性) in the ordinary usage does not, or does not yet, represent a general understanding or acceptance that the person's 'sex' (whatever one understands the word to mean) has really been 'changed'.

The Court of Appeal upheld the High Court decision by affirming that the *Corbett* approach that stresses the biological sex still represented the present state of law in Hong Kong. Concerning the notion of ordinary meaning, the judge Hon Fok JA quoted the principle that "a statute is treated as always speaking and the court should construe it in accordance with the need to treat it as continuing to operate as current law."[128] When deciding the "updated meaning" of the relevant terms, the court concluded that "the contemporary meaning of the words 'man' and 'woman' has not been shown to have expanded in ordinary, everyday usage to include a post-operative transsexual man or woman respectively."[129] The court also found that there is no evidence of societal consensus in Hong Kong regarding the right of transgender individuals to marry in any sex other than the sex assigned at birth.[130]

The Court of Final Appeal reversed the lower court decisions on the grounds of constitutional interpretation as stated in the Bill of Rights and the Basic

---

[125] *W. v. Registrar of Marriages* [2010] 6 HKC 359, para. 54.

[126] *W. v. Registrar of Marriages* [2010] 6 HKC 359, para. 139.

[127] *W. v. Registrar of Marriages* [2010] 6 HKC 359, para. 121.

[128] *W. v. Registrar of Marriages* [2012] 1 HKC 88, para. 73.

[129] *W. v. Registrar of Marriages* [2012] 1 HKC 88, para. 93.

[130] *W. v. Registrar of Marriages* [2012] 1 HKC 88, para. 142.

Law.[131] Even though the Court of Final Appeal ruled that the Registrar did not in principle misconstrue the Marriage Ordinance, it held that the *Corbett* criteria are incomplete given that they are limited to a person's biological features existing at the time of birth.[132] The court also suggested that the importance of procreation in marriage has much diminished and is no longer a legal requirement of marriage.[133] This court acknowledged the declining importance of chromosomal elements which was once believed to be decisive and unchallengeable. On the notion of societal consensus, the court treated the setup of "Gender Identity and Sexual Orientation Unit" and "Sexual Minorities Forum," a forum which aimed at handling gender identity and sexual orientation issues in 2005 by the Hong Kong government, as proofs of changes in societal attitudes towards transgender people in Hong Kong.[134] Having addressed the importance of purpose and context, it was not the court's intention to deal with the Marriage Registrar's statutory construction argument "that involved the textual argument that a post-operative male-to-female transsexual person cannot marry a man because she is not a 'woman' within the ordinary meaning of that term."[135] The court further added that "[t]he argument relied on the absence of evidence that the current ordinary usage of 'man', 'woman', 'male' and 'female' encompasses transsexuals; on the dictionary meanings of such words; and on the existence of negative attitudes towards transsexuals in Hong Kong."[136] The court decided not to take part in the arguments of ordinary meaning for "legislative intent made evident by their enactment history in the light of the *Corbett* decision" should be the court's main concern.[137] For the court, "[t]hat approach, in our view, leaves no room for a debate on 'ordinary meaning' nor on whether the 'always speaking' provisions deserve an updated meaning."[138] The court held that the application of the Corbett criteria would "impair the very essence of the right to marry"[139] and eventually held that a remedial interpretation should be given to the Marriage Ordinance that requires the references to "woman" and "female" to be read as capable of accommodating transgender people who have undergone gender confirmation surgery for marriage purposes.[140]

---

[131] *W. v. Registrar of Marriages* [2013] HKCFA 39; FACV4/2012.
[132] *W. v. Registrar of Marriages* [2013] HKCFA 39; FACV4/2012, para. 118.
[133] *W. v. Registrar of Marriages* [2013] HKCFA 39; FACV4/2012, para. 84.
[134] *W. v. Registrar of Marriages* [2013] HKCFA 39; FACV4/2012, para. 93.
[135] *W. v. Registrar of Marriages* [2013] HKCFA 39; FACV4/2012, para. 52.
[136] *W. v. Registrar of Marriages* [2013] HKCFA 39; FACV4/2012, para. 52.
[137] *W. v. Registrar of Marriages* [2013] HKCFA 39; FACV4/2012, para. 53.
[138] *W. v. Registrar of Marriages* [2013] HKCFA 39; FACV4/2012, para. 53.
[139] *W. v. Registrar of Marriages* [2013] HKCFA 39; FACV4/2012, para. 111.
[140] *W. v. Registrar of Marriages* [2013] HKCFA 39; FACV4/2012, .para. 123.

3.3.3 Finding the "Ordinary Meaning" of the Words "Woman" and "Female" in the Context of Hong Kong

In order to define a person's sex, the *Corbett* precedent's binary biological sex approach has once again influenced the High Court and the Court of Appeal decisions in *W.*, in which both courts have adopted this binary biological sex approach to interpret the ordinary meaning of the words "man" and "woman." Definitions from the *Shorter Oxford English Dictionary* (6th ed., 2007) were quoted by the High Court judge that defined the word "woman" as "an adult female person" and defined the adjective "female" as "of, pertaining to, or designating the sex whichh can beget offspring or produce eggs . . . ."[141] The judge further ruled that:

> [I]n Hong Kong, a post-operative transsexual individual is still generally referred to as such either in the English language or in the Chinese language (ie "變性人", "變性男人" or "變性女人"), rather than simply as a "man" ("男人") or a "woman" ("女人") in accordance with the post-operative gender acquired.[142]

The court further adopted a purposive approach in interpreting the statute since the judge held that it was important for the court to find out the intention of the legislature.[143] The purpose of the Ordinance was believed to be providing for "the celebration of Christian marriage" which required "marriage be the union of one man and one woman."[144] Furthermore, even though the judge noticed that an "updating construction" should be given to an ongoing Act, there was in fact a limit for the Act to be updated with regard to social changes.[145] For the judge, "[w]hat is not permitted is to alter the meaning of the words used in the enactment in ways which do not fall within the principles originally envisaged by the enactment."[146] Words, according to the judge, should be given their natural and ordinary meaning and the ordinary meaning of the words "man" and "woman" simply could not include a transgender man or women, even if they had undergone gender confirmation surgery. However, when reaching such conclusion, especially when it concerned the Chinese usage of the terms in Hong Kong society, no further sociological discussion was provided by the judge to illustrate how the ordinary usage of the relevant terms in ordinary English or Chinese is inferred, and it seems that the whole decision on the local

---

[141] *W.* v. *Registrar of Marriages* [2010],. para. 138.
[142] *W.* v. *Registrar of Marriages* [2010],.para. 140.
[143] *W.* v. *Registrar of Marriages* [2010], para. 106.
[144] *W.* v. *Registrar of Marriages* [2010],.paras. 109 and 113.
[145] *W.* v. *Registrar of Marriages* [2010],.para. 127.
[146] *W.* v. *Registrar of Marriages* [2010],.para. 127.

usage of Hong Kong's bilingual usage of the relevant terms is based on the judge's intuition (Hutton, 2019b).

The Court of Appeal upheld the High Court decision in its interpretation of the ordinary meaning of "woman" and "female." The importance of using the relevant words in both English and Chinese in the context of Hong Kong has been stressed by the court.[147] To support this, an academic article entitled "Finding a voice, fighting for rights: the emergence of the transgender movement in Hong Kong" (Emerton, 2006) was also quoted to explain the ordinary usage of the relevant words in Hong Kong. By quoting an article that was published in 2006, the court used the article to suggest a considerably hostile attitude that the society held against transgender people for the highly derogatory term that was transliterated as *yan yiu* (English word-for-word translation: human monster) was the commonly used Cantonese term that was used by the tabloid press to refer to a transgender person.[148] The term *yan yiu* in Cantonese signifies a person with monstrous characteristics and carries highly negative connotations. As suggested by Erni (2013), this term does "command a kind of cultural ubiquity that produces a sensation of shame and humiliation strong enough to induce self-policing" (p. 149). He further states that this term is "a language that pierces through the body, gender, and sexuality to perform a deeper social degradation of one's 'personal character'" (p. 149). For the Chinese-language broadsheets, a more neutral and nonderogatory term *bin sang yan* (English word-for-word translation: sex-changed person) was normally used in their news reports.[149] Emerton's article as was treated as "powerful reasons" for supporting the fact that the ordinary, everyday usage of the words "man," "woman," "male," and "female" fails to "refer to a transsexual man and woman, whether pre- or post-operative."[150] The reasoning behind this is that in Hong Kong, as suggested in Emerton's article, there were specific and different terminologies (e.g. *yan yiu* and *bin sang* yan) to describe transgender individuals. They are simply not called "male" or "female," or "man" or "woman," which made them under a different category. Despite the wide coverage of the contemporary Australian meaning of the words "man" and "woman" that cover transgender individuals who have undergone gender confirmation surgery, the Hong Kong court found that there is no sufficient evidence to support that "the contemporary Hong Kong meaning of those words includes a post-operative transsexual."[151] For "evidence" to support the updated meaning of the relevant

---

[147] *W.* v. *Registrar of Marriages* [2012], para. 73.
[148] *W.* v. *Registrar of Marriages* [2012], para 71.
[149] *W* v *Registrar of Marriages* [2012], para 71.
[150] *W.* v. *Registrar of Marriages* [2012], para. 92.
[151] *W.* v. *Registrar of Marriages* [2012], para. 100.

words in Hong Kong in the year of 2011, the year where the Court of Appeal delivered its decision in *W.*, Emerton's 2006 article was used as one of the major pieces of evidence.

Ms. Emerton's article was published in 2006 to document the Hong Kong transgender movement (Emerton, 2006). The author especially concentrated her research on the objectives and activities of the Hong Kong Transgender Equality and Acceptance Movement (TEAM), which was established in 2002 and was the first organized group of transgender people and supporters in Hong Kong (Emerton, 2006). With the purpose of helping transgender people to find their voice and fight for legal recognition, aspects regarding language and media portrayal of transgender people in the context of Hong Kong were analyzed. With such a background of the article in mind, the fact that Hong Kong Court of Appeal used this article to counter-argue the acceptance of transgender individuals in Hong Kong society is contradictory to the author's intention in support of transgender individuals and helping them to fight for their legal rights. This also poses another paradox between the author's motivation in advocating for transgender rights and the judges' usage of the article to illustrate the lack of societal support for transgender people's legal rights. In addition, the fact that Emerton's article was published in 2006 casts doubts on the suitability for this article to be used to speak for the context of Hong Kong in the year of 2011. Emerton's article was based on data mostly collected in 2005. Newspapers, including *The Sun*, *Oriental Daily*, and *Singpao*, which projected a negative image of transgender people by naming transgender people as *yan yiu* in 2005, were analyzed. However, when the *W.* case was out between the year of 2010–2013, nearly all of the Hong Kong newspapers and magazines, for instance *The Sun* (newspaper) and *Faces* (magazine), addressed Ms. W. as *bin sang yan* rather than *yan yiu*.[152] *Hong Kong Commercial Daily* (August 11, 2010) even used "W小姐" (English word-for-word translation: "Ms. W.") instead of *bin sang yan* to address her in the title of the news: "變性博士W小姐爭婚權" (English word-for-word translation: "Sex changed Doctor Ms W fights for the right to marry"). This indicates that the term *yan yiu* was rarely used by the Hong Kong press during the *W.* case period and considerable changes in how the press and society addressed transgender people were observed. The question remains as to where can an "updated meaning" of the ordinary usage and understanding of the relevant terms be obtained and put

---

[152] See Sing Pao (16/04/2011) "獨家專訪 盡訴真情 變性人誓再爭婚權" (Exclusive: Pouring herself out: *bin sang yan* (Sex Changed Person) is determined to fight for her right of marry again). Faces (13–10-2010) "結婚敗訴 獨家專訪變性人W: 老公喺巴士站溝我!" (Failed to get married Exclusive interview with as *bin sang yan* (Sex Changed Person) W: My husband courted me at the bus stop!).

more specifically, whether such a meaning can be obtained in a single source of reference.

3.3.4 From Searching for the Ordinary Meaning of the Relevant Terms to Considering Constitutional Issues

In an important shift, the Court of Final Appeal in *W.* did not consider it necessary to analyze or investigate the ordinary meaning of the word "woman" in marriage law, nor the current usage of the relevant words in the context of Hong Kong. Unlike the High Court and the Court of Appeal in *W.*, this court was not concerned about whether there was evidence to show that the ordinary usage of "man" and "woman" could encompass postoperative transgender individuals or whether the dictionary meanings of such words could represent the ordinary meaning of those terms.[153] The dictionary was evidently not the source of references that the judges turned to when dealing with the legal questions. Instead of focusing the reasoning on finding the ordinary meaning of the relevant words, the Court of Final Appeal emphasized constitutional questions, including the nature and importance of the constitutional right to marry as well as how procreation is no longer regarded as essential to marriage.[154] When deciding whether W. actually qualifies as "a woman" in marriage law, the court decision was that all the circumstances have to be considered, including biological, psychological and social. This *W.* Court of Final Appeal judgment shows us that the *Corbett* decision is no longer sufficient to speak for Hong Kong's legal context, and that the dictionary is no longer the ultimate answer as to a person's sex, since other factors should also be examined. It has brought recognition to Hong Kong transgender women who have undergone gender confirmation surgery, for their affirmed sex could be recognized in the marriage law. However, the court's approach of not engaging in arguments about ordinary meaning leads the question as to how Hong Kong society views a person's sex and whether the ordinary meaning of terms such as "woman" and "female" can encompass transgender individuals to be unanswered. No "updated meaning" of the relevant terms in 2013 was provided by the court. The court also only acknowledged the legal status of a transgender woman who has undergone gender confirmation surgery in marriage law, contributing to the formation of a legal discourse of a stereotypical understanding of transgender people. Such discourse points at the completion of gender confirmation surgery, which will result in an irreversible body transformation and the exclusion of other possibilities of gender representations (see Sharpe 1996, 2010; Hutton

---

[153] *W.* v. *Registrar of Marriages* [2013], para. 52.
[154] *W.* v. *Registrar of Marriages* [2013], paras. 67 and 86.

2011, 2019b; Tao 2016; Honkasalo 2020). This rather limited and fixed representation of transgender individuals could cause the space for the expression of gender fluidity and complexities to be narrowed, rendering some transgender individuals as legally and socially unintelligible.

3.4 Conclusion

When analyzing the transgender cases in marriage law, one can observe that there is a gradual legal development that changes the legal categorization and coverage of transgender individuals. *Corbett* was speaking on behalf of the 1970s, which established the framework of using "biological sex" to determine a person's sex. *Goodwin* marked the passing of the Gender Recognition Act in 2004 by the UK parliament, which allowed transgender people to change their legal sex and to marry in heterosexual relationships. For *Bellinger* and *W.* (High Court and Court of Appeal), to a large extent, they supported *Corbett*'s binary biological sex approach and treated *Corbett* as representing the state of law in their countries and regions. However, they also took factors such as ordinary meanings of the words "man," "woman," "male," and "female" into consideration. They were concerned about whether the statute's actual language had changed its meaning when interpreting those relevant words. This opened up the possibility that *Corbett* on its own was not enough to speak for the current social context and that at some point, the social context and consensus will change. Due to these factors, they then needed the ordinary meaning argument to back up their adoption of the *Corbett* decision and to make reference to the current social context and changes. The groundbreaking Court of Final Appeal judgment in *W.* drastically shifted from the *Corbett* and *Bellinger* decisions given that it highlighted changes in both medical and social understandings and recognized the importance of gender confirmation surgery. However, while the Hong Kong Court of Final Appeal of the *W.* case in 2013 suggested the Hong Kong government to consider other legal measures to protect Hong Kong transgender people, including the United Kingdom's Gender Recognition Act (2004), such a development and discussion still remain stagnant in Hong Kong society.

4 Conclusion

This Element discusses how transgender people are understood and categorized by the law within a particular legal framework. Layers of indeterminacy in the meaning of the words "man," "woman," "male," and "female" can be found when examining the legal interpretation of these terms in Title VII and marriage law. The judges in those cases consulted different sources of authority such as precedents, medical experts, societal views, and institutional evidence when finding the "plain language" and "ordinary meaning" of the relevant words. All of these factors have contributed to judges' searches of the most suitable meaning of the words in the indexical field (Eckert 2008; Calder 2021). An analysis of different judges' statutory interpretation processes reveals to us the fluidity and dynamic nature of the links between words and objects (which bodies and individuals can be seen as "women" in law). It further points to the importance of context for all the statutory wordings need to be construed in a specific context (e.g. the jurisdiction) by a specific perceiver (e.g. the judge(s)), resulting in different interpretations of the same terms such as "sex," "man," and "woman." For courts in *Holloway*, *Ulane II*, *Corbett*, and *Bellinger*, biological sex remains to be the ultimate answer to one's sex. For the more progressive judgments such as those in *Ulane I*, *Smith*, *Schroer*, *Bostock*, and *W.* (Court of Final Appeal), a broader interpretation of construing the statute for protecting transgender individuals was introduced. However, this broader interpretation does not necessarily invite a rejection to the long-standing "biological sex" approach and still maintains a fixed gender binary distinction between men and women, rendering transgender people who do not wish to conform to either male or female gender roles unprotected. This is particularly obvious in the case of *Ulane I* and *W.* (Court of Final Appeal) where the gender confirmation surgery itself is suggested to be the essential step in validating transgender individuals' affirmed gender identity. Sharpe (1996) suggests that in law, psychological sex can only be established through surgical intervention for "coherent" gender identity in law needs to be linked to the state of genitalia (Sharpe, 1996). Even though the *Corbett* approach has been rejected by some of the courts, it seems that the body itself continues to speak of a person's sex. The discussion in this Element also indicates that it would be nearly impossible to have a single and fixed definition of the words "man" and "woman" as well as the concept of "sex" because they are highly complex terms that are embedded in multiple personal and social realities. Hong Kong, with its complex legal background and stagnant discussion on a possible Gender Recognition Act, also seems to be facing systemic challenges in introducing a more comprehensive legal protection for all different types of transgender individuals. For transgender individuals in Hong Kong, if one does not undergo the gender confirmation surgery, the individual will then be regarded as incomprehensible from the legal perspective.

Foucault (1978) views the relationship between law and sex as repressive, since law is understood as constituting reality, desires, and sex and using its power to suppress or control. Davies (1997) also holds that "there is a social law – not a natural law – which forces sex upon us. As subjects of this law, we must be sexed, we cannot escape being one thing or the other" (p. 33). Even though law sets limits on its subjects and establishes a specific framework for viewing its subjects, it also allows its subjects to be presented and understood by the society. The above legal analysis shows that law is progressing towards legally recognizing transgender people's (in most cases, transgender people who have undergone gender confirmation surgery) affirmed sex. Take *Corbett* and *W.* as an example, the delivery of the judgments created a whole domain of discussion across the notion of transgender phenomenon in the society. These discussions permeate different sectors of society and have led to increased emphasis in the public sphere on transgender issues, including their legal rights, predicaments, and stories. For the future legal development in protecting transgender individuals, an important direction is to go beyond the coverage of only those who conform to a binary gender distinction and have undergone the gender confirmation surgery. Instead of viewing legal subjects as merely passive, it is believed that transgender people hold the ability to take part in reshaping the dominant gender ideologies in society and in law. They can exemplify the conception of postmodernity by breaking people away from the rigid understanding of dichotomy (Stryker, 2006). In postmodern understandings, fluidity predominates, and identity boundaries are held to be fictions of modernity that are open for negotiation and construction (Hutton, 2019b).

For this to be achieved, it is important to address how transgender people are constantly playing a rather passive role in the issue of legal definition. A portion of the existing work on queer linguistics used a community of practice model to investigate the production and contestation of normativity within groups that may or may not hold uniformity in identity formation (e.g. Bucholtz, 1999; Mendoza-Denton, 1999). Such a production and contestation of normativity can be reflected in how judges in transgender cases have maintained the gender binary and excluded non-operative transgender individuals in law, presenting only the courts' viewpoint to the public. The queer linguistics approach, however, reminds us to be critical with such a circulating and one-sided view of normativity, for one of the aims of queer linguistics is to reveal and problematize normative and restricting gender and sexuality ideologies. King (2016, p. 361) states that when arguing bodies are discursively constructed, it is "not to suggest that they are not important," but instead that "the relationship between bodies and discourse is one of co-construction." The legal discourse that constructs specific gendered bodies as legally and socially intelligible while some as unintelligible shows that law is undeniably controlling and shaping one form of sex and gender ideologies and understanding. However, on top of legal discourse, it is also equally if not more important for transgender individuals' voices to be heard in the process of constructing (trans)gender ideologies and understanding in law. Zimman (2014) and King (2016) both discuss the creative linguistic means of articulating one's genitalia, a means that could bring the lowest level of discomfort to transgender individuals. Konnelly (2021) further suggests that trans individuals have the ability to use language in creative and strategic ways, implying that speakers can "dialogically construct different types of embodiment depending on the context" (Jones, 2022). How transgender individuals can take part in the meaning construction process and contribute to the establishment of an indexical link between linguistic sign and objects in courts will be of paramount importance in to the "co-construction" process of both discourse and bodies in law and society. Vade (2015, p. 278) calls for an expansion of legal space to accommodate the "gender galaxy," a term that he refers to as "a space with many genders," because failing to do so would cause many different gender nonconforming individuals to be impossible in the law. Life can resist power and brings in other possibilities. The seemingly fixed understanding of a person's sex needs to be questioned and expanded while the exclusion of all forms of transgender individuals' voices in law has to be addressed to further protect and allow different gender possibilities in law.

References

Aprill, E. P. (1998). The law of the word: Dictionary shopping in the Supreme Court. *Arizona State Law Journal*, *30*, 277–336.

Atkin, A. (2013). Peirce's theory of signs. In E. N. Zalta (Ed.), *The Stanford encyclopedia of philosophy* (Summer 2013 Edition).

Bannet, E. T. (1997). The Marriage Act of 1753: 'a most cruel law for the fair sex'. *Eighteenth Century Studies*, *30*(3), 233–254.

Beyer, D., Weiss, J. T. & Wilchins, R. (2014). New Title VII and EEOC Rulings Protect Transgender Employees. http://transgenderlawcenter.org/wp-content /uploads/2014/01/TitleVII-Report-Final012414.pdf.

Bolin, A. (1994). Transcending and transgendering: Male-to-female transsexuals, dichotomy and diversity. In G. Herdt (Ed.), *Third sex, third gender: Beyond sexual dimorphism in culture and history* (pp. 447–485). Zone Books.

Bourdieu, P. (1987). The force of law: Toward a sociology of the juridical field. *The Hastings Law Journal*, *38*(5), 814–853.

Broadus, K. W. (2006). The evolution of employment discrimination protections for transgender people. In P. Currah, R. M. Juang & S. P. Minter (Eds.), *Transgender rights* (pp. 93–101). University of Minnesota Press.

Bucholtz, M. (1999) "Why be normal?" Language and identity practices in a community of Nerd girls. *Language in Society*, *28*(2), 203–223.

Butler, J. (1993). *Bodies that matter: On the discursive limits of "sex."* Routledge. Butler, J. (1998). Subjects of sex/gender/desire. In S. Kemp & J. Squires (Eds.), *Feminisms* (pp. 278–285). Oxford University Press.

Butler, J. (1999). Revisiting bodies and pleasures. *Theory, Culture & Society*, *16*(2), 11–20.

Calder, J. (2021). Whose indexical field is it? The role of community epistemology in indexing social meaning. *Proceedings of the 20th Meeting of the Texas Linguistics Society*, March 5–6, pp. 39–55. http://tls.ling.utexas.edu/ 2021tls/TLS_2021_Proceedings.pdf.

Cheung, K. (2016). The 'bathroom hurdle': A transgender woman's fight for legal recognition and safe spaces. *Hong Kong Free Press*. https://hon gkongfp.com/2016/05/29/the-bathroom-hurdle-a-transgender-womans-fight-for-legal-recognition-and-safe-spaces/1/18.

Chow, Y. (2013, July, 13). Hong Kong must do right by its transgender minority. *South China Morning Post*. www.scmp.com/comment/insight-opinion/article/1280403/hong-kong-must-do-right-its-transgender-minority.

Cunningham, C. D., Levi, J. N., Green, G. M. & Kaplant, J. P. (1993). Plain meaning and hard cases. *The Yale Law Journal, 103*(6), 1561–1625.

Currah, P. & Minterm, S. (2000). Unprincipled exclusions: The struggle to achieve judicial and legislative equality for transgender people. *William & Mary Journal of Women and the Law, 7*(1), 37–66.

Davies, M. (1997). Taking the inside out: Sex and gender in the legal subject. In N. Naffine & R. J. Owens (Eds.), *Sexing the subject of law* (pp. 25–46). LBC Information Services.

Deleuze, G., & Guattari, F. (1988). Thousand plateaus: Capitalism and schizophrenia (B. Massumi, Trans.). Athlone.

D'Onofrio, Annette. (2021). Sociolinguistic signs as cognitive representations. In L. Hall-Lew, E. Moore & R. Podesva (Eds.), *Social meaning in linguistic variation: Theorizing the third wave* (pp. 153–175). Cambridge University Press.

Eckert, P. (2008). Variation and the indexical field. *Journal of Sociolinguistics, 12*(4), 453–476.

Emerton, R. (2006). Finding a voice, fighting for rights: The emergence of the transgender movement in Hong Kong. *Inter-Asia Cultural Studies, 7*(2), 243–269.

Erni, J. N. (2013). Legitimating transphobia: The legal disavowal of transgender rights in prison. *Cultural Studies, 27*(1), 136–159.

Eskridge, W. N. (1994). *Dynamic statutory interpretation*. Harvard University Press.

Evan, J. (1988). *Statutory interpretation: Problems of communication*. Oxford University Press.

Fallon Jr, R. H. (2014). Three symmetries between textualist and purposivist theories of statutory interpretation – and the irreducible roles of values and judgment within both. *Cornell Law Review, 99*(4), 685–734.

Feldman, S. M. (1996). The politics of postmodern jurisprudence. *Michigan Law Review, 95*(1), 166–202.

Feldman, S. M. (2000). How to be critical. *Chicago-Kent Law Review, 76*(893), 893–912.

Ferrara, A. (1993). *Modernity and authenticity: A study of the social and ethical thought of Jean-Jacques Rousseau*. State University of New York Press.

Fish, S. (1987). Still wrong after all these years. *Law and Philosophy, 6*(3), 401–418.

Fish, S. (1989). *Doing what comes naturally: Change, rhetoric, and the practice of theory in literary and legal studies*. Clarendon Press.

Foucault, M. (1978). *The history of sexuality: An introduction volume 1*. (R. Hurley, Trans.). Vintage Books.

Foucault, M. (1980). *Hercule barbin*. Pantheon.

Fuller, L. (1967). *Legal fictions*. Stanford University Press.

Gal, S. & Irvine, J. T. (2019). *Signs of difference: Language and ideology in social life*. Cambridge University Press.

Goodrich, P. (1996). Gender and contract. In A. Bottomley (Ed.), *Feminist perspectives on The foundational subjects of law* (pp. 17–46). Cavendish Publishing Limited.

Gorsuch, N. (2019). *A republic, if you can keep it*. Forum Books.

Green, R. (1985). Spelling "relief" for transsexuals: Employment discrimination and the criteria of sex. *Yale Law & Policy Review*, *4*(1), 125–140.

Grove, T. L. (2020). Which textualism? *Harvard Law Review*, *134*, 265–307.

Harris, R. (1998). *Introduction to integrational linguistics*. Pergamon.

Hart, H. L. A. (1994). *The concept of law* (2nd ed., first published in 1961). Clarendon Press.

Hill-Collins, P. (1990). *Black feminist thought: Knowledge, consciousness, and the politics of empowerment*. Routledge.

Honkasalo, J. (2020). In the shadow of eugenics: Transgender sterilization legislation and the struggle for self-determination. In K. Gupta, D. L. Steinberg, I. Moon, & R. Pearce (Eds.), *The emergence of trans: Cultures, politics and everyday lives* (pp. 17–31). Routledge.

Hooley, J. (1994). What is this thing called Gender "Dysphoria"? Tranys with attitude, 6–11, *The Newsletter of the Transgender Liberation Coalition*.

Hutton, C. (2011). Objectification and transgender jurisprudence: The dictionary as quasi-statute. *Hong Kong Law Journal*, *41*, 27–47.

Hutton, C. (2014a). *Word, meaning and legal interpretation: An introductory guide*. Palgrave Macmillan.

Hutton, C. (2014b). The tangle of colonial modernity: Hong Kong as a distinct linguistic and conceptual space within the global common law. *Law Text Culture*, *8*, 221–248.

Hutton, C. (2017). Transgender jurisprudence: Legal sex and ordinary language. In E. Hazenberg & M. Meyerhoff (Eds.), *Representing Trans: Linguistic, Legal and Everyday Perspectives* (pp. 55–76). Victoria University Press.

Hutton, C. (2009). *Language, meaning and the law*. Edinburgh: Edinburgh University Press.

Hutton, C. (2019a). *Integrationism and the self: Reflections on the legal personhood of animals*. London: Routledge.

Jones, L. (2022). 'I'm a boy, can't you see that?': Dialogic embodiment and the construction of agency in trans youth discourse. *Language in Society*, 1–22. https://doi.org/10.1017/S0047404522000252.

Hutton, C. (2019b). *The tyranny of ordinary meaning: Corbett v Corbett and legal sex*. Palgrave.

King, B. W. (2016). Becoming the intelligible Other: Speaking intersex bodies against the grain. *Critical Discourse Studies, 13*(4), 359–378.

King, M. (2003). Research and discussion paper: Perceptions of MtF transgendered persons and their sexual partners in Hong Kong. http://web.hku.hk/~sjwinter/TransgenderASIA/paperperceptions_of_mtf.htm.

Konnelly, L. (2021). Nuance and normativity in trans linguistic research. *Journal of Language and Sexuality, 10*(1), 71–82.

Latour, B. (1993). *We have never been modern*. Harvard University Press.

Lin, Z. (2020, November 13). 香港罕有跨性別武術家許瑋楓專訪:「我男變女, 喜歡女生, 一點不柔弱」 [Interview with Transgender Martial Artist Hui Wai Fung in Hong Kong: "I transitioned from male to female, I am in love women, and I'm not at all weak"]. *BBC News*. www.bbc.com/zhongwen/trad/chinese-news- 54553312.

Manning, J. F. (2006). What divides textualists from purposivists? *Columbia Law Review, 106*(1), 70–111.

Melvin, A. E. (1988). *The nature of the common law*. Harvard University Press.

Mendoza-Denton, N. (1999). Fighting words: Latina girls, gangs, and language attitudes. In D. L. Galindo & M. D. Gonzales (Eds.), *Speaking Chicana: Voice, power, and identity* (pp. 39–56). University of Arizona Press.

Nakassis, C. (2018). Indexicality's ambivalent ground. *Signs and Society, 6*(1), 281–304.

Ormrod, R. (1972). The medico-legal aspects of sex determination. *The Medico-Legal Journal, 40*(3), 18–32.

Rosch, E. (1999). Principles of categorization. In E. Margolis and S. Laurence (Eds.), *Concepts: Core readings* (pp. 189–206). Massachusetts Institute of Technology Press.

Royal Anthropological Institute (RAI). (1951). *Notes and queries on anthropology* (6th ed.). Royal Anthropological Institute.

Rynd, A. J. (1991). Dictionaries and the interpretation of words: A summary of difficulties. *Alberta Law Review, 28*, 712–717.

Scalia, A. (1997). *A matter for interpretation: Federal courts and the law*. Princeton University Press.

Schauer, F. (1989). [Review of the book *The nature of the common law* by A. E. Melvin]. Is the common law law? *California Law Review, 77*(2), 455–471.

Silverstein, M. (1985). Language and the culture of gender: At the intersection of structure, usage and ideology. In E. Mertz & R. Parmentier (Eds.), *Semiotic mediation: Sociocultural and psychological perspectives* (pp. 219–259). Academic Press.

Silverstein, M. (2003). Indexical order and the dialectics of sociolinguistic life. *Language and Communication, 23*(3–4), 193–229.

Smith, C. (2000). The sovereign state v Foucault: Law and disciplinary power. *The Sociological Review, 48*(2), 283–306. https://doi.org/10.1111/1467-954X.00216

Schwartz, J. (2009). *In pursuit of the gene: From Darwin to DNA.* Harvard University Press.

Sharpe A. (1996). Judicial uses of transsexuality: A site for political contestation. *AlternativeL. J., 21*, 153–172.

Sharpe, A. (2002). *Transgender jurisprudence: Dysphoric bodies of law.* Cavendish Pub.

Sharpe A. (2010). *Foucault's monsters and the challenge of law.* Routledge.

Solan, L. (1993). *The language of judges.* University of Chicago Press.

Solan, L. (1995). Judicial decisions and linguistic analysis: Is there a linguist in the court?. *Washington University Law Quarterly, 73*, 1069–80.

Solan, L, (2010). The language of statutes. The University of Chicago Press.

Stryker, S. (2006). (De)subjugated knowledges. In S. Stryker & S. Whittle (Eds.), *The Transgender studies reader* (pp. 1–18). Routledge.

Suen, Y. T., Chan, R. C.H. & Wong, E. M. Y. (2021). Excluded lives: The largest scale survey on the social and legal marginalisation of transgender people in Hong Kong so far. [Report]. Sexualities Research Programme, Chinese University of Hong Kong.

Taylor, C. (1989). Sources of the self. The making of the modern identity. Cambridge University Press.

Tao K. W. Y. (2016). Exploring the sources of authority over the word meaning in transgender jurisprudence. *Marginalised Bodies (Re)Imagining the Law,* Special Issue for *International Journal for the Semiotics of Law, 29*, 29–44.

Tao, K. W. Y. (2022). Claiming transgender identity: Contextualising the linguistic tension among trans women in Hong Kong. *Gender and Language* (special issue).

Transgender Equality Hong Kong. (2021). *Transgender people in the workplace.* http://www.tehk.org.hk/.

Vade, D. (2004). Expanding gender and expanding the law: Toward a social and legal conceptualization of gender that is more inclusive of transgender people. *Michigan Journal of Gender and Law, 11*, 253–313.

Weiss, J. T. (2008) Transgender identity, textualism, and the Supreme Court: What is the "plain meaning" of "sex" in Title VII of the Civil Rights Act of 1964?. *Temple Political &Civil Rights Law Review. 18*(2), 573–650.

Werbach, K. (1994). Looking it up: Dictionaries and statutory interpretation. *Harvard Law Review, 107*, 1437–53.

Willis, H. (1926). A definition of law. *Virginia Law Review, 12*, 203–214.

Wittgenstein, L. (1978). Philosophical investigations (G.E.M. Anscombe, Trans.). Blackwell.

Zander, M. (2004). The law-making process (6th ed.). Cambridge University Press.

Zimman, L. (2014). The discursive construction of sex: Remaking and reclaiming the gendered body in talk about genitals among trans men. In L. Zimman, J. L. Davis, & J. Raclaw (Eds.), *Queer excursions: Rethinking binaries in language, gender, and sexuality* (pp. 13–34). Oxford University Press.

Cambridge Elements ≡

Language, Gender and Sexuality

Elements in the Series

The Language of Gender-Based Separatism
Veronika Koller, Alexandra Krendel, and Jessica Aiston

Queering Sexual Health Translation Pedagogy
Piero Toto

Legal Categorization of "Transgender": An Analysis of Statutory Interpretation of "Sex", "Man", and "Woman" in Transgender Jurisprudence
Kimberly Tao

A full series listing is available at: www.cambridge.org/ELGS

Printed in the United States
by Baker & Taylor Publisher Services